Alan R. Moon

TICKET TO RIDE™

THE OFFICIAL COOKBOOK

RECIPES INSPIRED BY
THE WORLD'S BEST-SELLING TRAIN GAME

ULYSSES PRESS

To all the intrepid travelers, strategists, and adventurers who have embarked on countless railway journeys in the world of Ticket to Ride.

....

Special thanks to Alan R. Moon; Adrien Martinot at Days of Wonder; and Katha Busk, Danielle Robb, and Alexander Thieme at Asmodee Entertainment.

Published by:
ULYSSES PRESS
PO Box 3440
Berkeley, CA 94703
www.ulyssespress.com

ISBN: 978-1-64604-497-9
Library of Congress Control Number: 2023930763

Printed in China
2 4 6 8 10 9 7 5 3 1

Cover design: Amy King
Interior design and layout: Jake Flaherty Design
Ticket to Ride artwork: Julien Delval
Photographs and recipes: Allyson Reedy and Greg McBoat

CONTENTS

Midwest

DESTINATION TICKET: SAULT STE. MARIE–OKLAHOMA CITY

MIDWEST MAIL Oklahoma City–Kansas City–Omaha

GREAT LAKES ZEPHYR Sault Ste. Marie–Duluth–Chicago

West

DESTINATION TICKET: VANCOUVER–SANTA FE

PACIFIC BEACHCOMBER Los Angeles–San Francisco

REDWOOD ZIPPER Portland–Seattle–Vancouver

DESTINATION TICKET: CALGARY–PHOENIX

ROCKY MOUNTAIN EAGLE Denver–Helena–Calgary

DESERT LIMITED Salt Lake City–Las Vegas–Los Angeles

DESTINATION TICKET: LOS ANGELES–MIAMI
SOUTHWEST EXPRESS Phoenix–El Paso–Santa Fe

TEXAS STAR El Paso–Houston–Dallas

COAST TO COAST
DESTINATION TICKET: VANCOUVER–MONTREAL
MAPLE LEAF Vancouver–Montreal

DESTINATION TICKET: NEW YORK–LOS ANGELES
CROSS-COUNTRY ROCKET New York–Los Angeles

INTRODUCTION

All aboard, hungry travelers!

You most likely already know Ticket to Ride™—the beloved cross-country train game that takes pluck, strategy, and an appetite for adventure. Players embark on new expeditions for every game, competing to connect different North American cities by rail and claim victory over fellow passengers. And what better way to explore a diverse, intriguing landscape than through its regional food and drink?

Just as the game takes you through the United States and Canada by rail, this cookbook gives you a culinary tour, focusing on regional recipes that will make completing your routes more delicious than ever. Those who love Ticket to Ride know that each game is new and exciting, an opportunity to not just connect cities and routes, but to connect with friends and family.

So while you're out exploring the map, cutting off your fellow continent-trotters' routes, punching tickets, and racing to travel through as many North American cities as possible, take that full-steam-ahead wanderlust to another level via these can't-lose snacks, desserts, meals, and drinks. All of them are strongly rooted in the cities featured in the game.

Recipes are organized by the Destination Tickets you know and love from the core Ticket to Ride game, featuring unique dining-car menus inspired by the cities through which you travel. Think of Hot Chicken in Nashville, New York's signature cheesecake, the Mai Tai that put a San Francisco bar on the map, and California's namesake sushi roll. Each of the 15 routes includes an appetizer, a side dish, a main course, a dessert, and a cocktail (with or without alcohol)—all with deliciously strong ties to destination cities.

As in the game itself, not all routes are created equal. Two Destination Tickets, the Cross-Country Rocket and the Maple Leaf, are especially long and varied, traversing North America and Canada, respectively. These longer routes stretch across the entire country, fueling riders up for a full day of adventure with such offerings as a Canadian breakfast of beaver tail pastries with real maple syrup and an all-American apple pie for dessert.

The recipes are as colorful as the game itself, spanning sweet to savory, vegetarian to meaty, and simple to skilled. All you need is an intrepid willingness to get in the kitchen, a stovetop, maybe a couple of bowls, and—of course—a healthy sprinkling of competitive spirit.

For new and experienced travelers alike, *Ticket to Ride: The Official Cookbook* will get you on track for a tasty game night.

EAST

DESTINATION TICKET

MONTREAL  ATLANTA

PITTSBURGH SALAD

A few things in a Pittsburgh salad are up for debate. You can use romaine or iceberg lettuce, grilled chicken or steak, and whatever veggies you want to throw in. The nonnegotiable? French fries. Without crunchy, salty fries, this salad is totally derailed. Thanks to Pittsburgh, you may never make a fry-less salad again.

Makes: 4 servings
Active time: 20 minutes
Total time: 1 hour 25 minutes

1 pound skirt steak

¼ cup olive oil

juice of ½ lemon

salt and pepper, to taste

1 cup frozen thin-cut french fries

3 cups lettuce (romaine or iceberg mix)

1 cucumber, sliced

2 carrots, peeled and shredded

½ cup sliced cherry tomatoes

½ cup croutons

¼ cup shredded cheddar cheese

RANCH DRESSING

½ cup sour cream

⅓ cup buttermilk

2 tablespoons mayonnaise

1 teaspoon dried dill

1 teaspoon dried parsley

1 teaspoon minced chives

½ teaspoon onion powder

1 clove garlic, minced

1 to 2 teaspoons fresh lemon juice

salt and pepper, to taste

1. Place the steak in a ziplock bag with the olive oil, lemon juice, salt, and pepper. Rub to distribute evenly, then refrigerate for at least an hour.

2. After the steak has marinated, sear it in a hot medium-size skillet over medium-high heat. For a medium-rare steak, cook the first side for 2 to 3 minutes, then flip and cook the second side for 1 to 2 minutes. Let rest for 4 minutes and then cut in thin slices.

3. Cook the french fries according to the package directions until crispy. Meanwhile, make the ranch dressing. In a small bowl, whisk together the sour cream, buttermilk, mayonnaise, dill, parsley, chives, onion powder, garlic, lemon juice, salt, and pepper.

4. To assemble the salad, place the lettuce in a large bowl and top with the cucumber slices, shredded carrots, cherry tomatoes, croutons, shredded cheese, fries, and steak. Drizzle with ranch dressing.

Hot Chicken

Nashville's best-known poultry is sweet, spicy, crispy, and juicy. After the chicken is fried to a perfect golden brown, it's slathered in a coating made from leftover frying oil, cayenne pepper, chili powder, and brown sugar. This combo of sweet and spicy ingredients is sure to make things steamy as your route takes you through Tennessee.

Makes: 4 servings
Active time: 40 minutes
Total time: 2 hours 40 minutes

1½ cups dill pickle juice

8 or so bone-in, skin-on chicken pieces (thighs, breasts, legs, wings)

2 cups flour

¼ cup cornstarch

3 tablespoons Creole seasoning

1½ cups buttermilk

⅓ cup Southern-style hot sauce, such as Frank's RedHot

2 quarts neutral oil, such as peanut or vegetable

⅓ cup ground cayenne pepper

1 tablespoon smoked paprika

1 tablespoon light or dark brown sugar

2 teaspoons chili powder

1 teaspoon garlic powder

1 teaspoon salt

1. Pour the pickle juice into a large ziplock bag. Add the chicken pieces and let them sit in the brine in the refrigerator for at least 2 hours, or up to overnight.

2. Set out two shallow dishes. In the first, mix together the flour, cornstarch, and Creole seasoning. In the second, pour the buttermilk and hot sauce.

3. Dunk each chicken piece into the flour mixture, then the buttermilk mixture, then back in the flour mixture. Place the breaded pieces on a wire rack set on a baking sheet.

4. Pour the oil into a large pot—it should come about a third to halfway up the pot sides—and heat over high heat until the oil reaches 350°F. (To check the temperature, use a cooking thermometer dipped into the oil or clipped to the side of the pot.)

5. Use tongs to carefully place half the chicken pieces in the oil. Fry for 7 to 10 minutes, depending on the size of the pieces (small thighs will cook faster than large breasts). Repeat with the remaining chicken pieces, then turn off the heat.

6. To make the spicy oil for the chicken, transfer at least a cup of the used cooking oil into a heatproof bowl. Add the cayenne pepper, paprika, brown sugar, chili powder, garlic powder, and salt, then mix everything together. Use a brush to coat the cooked chicken pieces with the spicy oil.

MAC AND CHEESE

Mac and cheese may very well be the end-all, be-all of American comfort foods. Perfected in the South but beloved by riders from all over, this dish is sure to garner a winning reaction on game night. Noodles coated in creamy, golden cheese cook evenly under a delectable crispy crust.

Makes: 12 servings
Active time: 20 minutes
Total time: 50 minutes

1 pound elbow macaroni

8 tablespoons (1 stick) unsalted butter, divided

⅓ cup flour

3½ cups whole milk

1 cup heavy whipping cream

4 cups shredded sharp cheddar cheese, divided

2 cups shredded parmesan cheese, divided

1 tablespoon onion powder

1 tablespoon garlic powder

1 teaspoon Creole seasoning

salt and pepper, to taste

1 cup panko breadcrumbs

½ teaspoon paprika

1. Preheat the oven to 350°F. Position one rack in the middle of the oven and another rack at the top. Cook the macaroni on the stovetop in boiling water according to package directions until just tender and shy of al dente. (The noodles will cook further in the oven.) Drain.

2. In a large saucepan over medium-low heat, melt 5 tablespoons of the butter. Stir or whisk in the flour and continue stirring for 1 to 2 minutes.

3. Stir or whisk in the milk and cream and continue stirring for 2 more minutes, until smooth. Turn the heat up to medium and gradually mix in 3 cups cheddar and 1½ cups parmesan cheese. Add the onion powder, garlic powder, Creole seasoning, salt, and pepper. Stir or whisk until smooth.

4. Pour the cooked macaroni into your cheese sauce and stir until well coated. Pour into a 3- or 4-quart baking dish and top with the remaining 1 cup cheddar cheese.

5. Melt the remaining 3 tablespoons butter in a small pan, then mix it with the panko, remaining ½ cup parmesan, and paprika. Sprinkle the mixture over the top of the mac and cheese.

6. On a rack positioned in the middle of the oven, bake for 20 to 25 minutes, until golden. Then turn the oven to broil and move the mac and cheese to the rack in the top position. Broil the mac and cheese for about 2 minutes, until it is just starting to brown. Serve while hot.

PEACHES AND CREAM CRISP

Georgia may be known as the Peach State, but peaches thrive throughout much of the Appalachian region, thanks to its sunny weather and fertile soil. While these rosy, juicy fruits are fantastic on their own, they're even better when coated in brown sugar and topped with cinnamon streusel and whipped cream. If you're playing with riders who have a sweet tooth, be sure to grab a serving fast or you'll be out of luck well before your fellow players are out of plastic train pieces.

Makes: 8 servings
Active time: 20 minutes
Total time: 1 hour

PEACHES

6 to 8 peaches, peeled, cored, and sliced (5 to 6 cups)

¼ cup light or dark brown sugar

2 tablespoons unsalted butter, melted

2 tablespoons flour

1 teaspoon lemon juice

1 teaspoon vanilla extract

1 teaspoon ground cinnamon

TOPPING

¾ cup flour

¾ cup old-fashioned rolled oats

¾ cup packed light or dark brown sugar

½ cup cold unsalted butter, cubed

¾ teaspoon baking powder

½ teaspoon ground cinnamon

¼ teaspoon ground nutmeg

½ teaspoon salt

WHIPPED CREAM

1 cup cold heavy whipping cream

2 tablespoons powdered sugar

½ teaspoon vanilla extract

1. Preheat the oven to 350°F. Place the sliced peaches in a large bowl. (Frozen peaches work fine if fresh ones aren't available.) Add the ¼ cup brown sugar, melted butter, flour, lemon juice, 1 teaspoon vanilla, and 1 teaspoon cinnamon. Toss to coat the peaches.

2. For the topping, in a separate bowl combine the flour, oats, ¾ cup brown sugar, cubed butter, baking powder, ½ teaspoon cinnamon, nutmeg, and salt. Using a pastry cutter (or your hands), form into a crumbly mixture. Refrigerate until ready to use.

3. Grease a 9 x 13-inch dish and pour in the peaches. Remove the topping mixture from the refrigerator and spread it over the peaches. Then bake for 35 to 45 minutes, until the top is golden and set.

4. To prepare the whipped cream, pour the cream, powdered sugar, and ½ teaspoon vanilla into a large chilled bowl. Whip on medium-high speed with an electric mixer for 3 to 4 minutes, until medium peaks form. Scoop onto the peach crisp servings.

NASHVILLE BUSHWACKER

This adult milkshake originated in the Caribbean using dark rum, but Nashville has taken over the Bushwacker as its party drink of choice, so of course they're all about the whiskey. Almost like a chocolaty piña colada, the shot of coffee liqueur gives it a different sort of buzz. Top it with whipped cream and freshly grated nutmeg for the ultimate in boozy indulgence to celebrate your victory—or to soften the blow of defeat.

> Makes: 2 drinks
> Total time: 5 minutes

1 cup ice

1 ounce (2 tablespoons) dark rum or whiskey

1 ounce (2 tablespoons) coffee liqueur

1 ounce (2 tablespoons) crème de cacao or dark chocolate liqueur

2 ounces (¼ cup) cream of coconut

2 ounces (¼ cup) whole milk

whipped cream, for topping

freshly ground nutmeg, for garnish

maraschino cherries, for garnish (optional)

1. In a blender, combine the ice, rum, coffee liqueur, crème de cacao, cream of coconut, and milk; blend until smooth.

2. Pour into two chilled glasses and top with whipped cream, freshly grated nutmeg, and cherry, if using.

Did You Know?

Ticket to Ride was first published in 2004. Later that year it won the prestigious Spiel des Jahres Board Game of the Year award.

TOASTED RAVIOLI

What could be better than fried cheese? How about fried cheese encased in pasta and served with a Calabrian chile–spiked marinara sauce? St. Louis knows what's up. That's where toasted ravioli—known there as T-Ravs—was popularized. This Italian-American recipe is great for snacking, and the crisp, golden ravioli filled with melted cheese is sure to please any game-playing crowd.

Makes: 6 servings
Active time: 30 minutes
Total time: 1 hour

1 cup whole milk

2 eggs

1 cup Italian breadcrumbs

1 teaspoon chopped fresh parsley

1 teaspoon dried oregano

½ teaspoon garlic powder

½ teaspoon onion powder

1 pound frozen cheese ravioli

2 tablespoons extra-virgin olive oil

3 cloves garlic, thinly sliced

1 tablespoon chopped Calabrian chiles or red pepper flakes

2 cups jarred marinara sauce

2 quarts vegetable oil

salt and pepper, to taste

¼ cup grated parmesan cheese

¼ cup chopped fresh parsley

1. In a shallow bowl, whisk milk and eggs to combine.

2. In another shallow bowl, stir together the breadcrumbs, parsley, oregano, garlic powder, and onion powder. Dip the ravioli pieces into the egg mixture and then into the breadcrumb mixture, coating both sides completely.

3. Place the breaded ravioli on a baking sheet lined with parchment paper, making sure they do not touch. Place in the freezer for 30 minutes.

4. In a small saucepan, combine the olive oil, garlic, and Calabrian chiles or pepper flakes and cook over medium-high heat for about 2 minutes, until the garlic just begins to brown. Add in the marinara sauce and turn the heat down to low. Simmer for at least 10 minutes, until the mixture is warmed through.

5. Meanwhile, fill a large pot with the vegetable oil and heat it on the stovetop to 350°F. Remove the ravioli from the freezer. Working in small batches, fry the ravioli in the oil for 3 to 4 minutes per batch. Place the cooked ravioli on a plate lined with paper towels and season with a sprinkling of salt and pepper, parmesan cheese, and fresh parsley. Serve with the warm sauce on the side in a small bowl.

SHRIMP PO' BOY

What makes a po' boy a po' boy? Crisp French bread, a creamy and slightly spicy remoulade sauce, and some form of protein—often fried shrimp. If your Destination Ticket allows you to route through New Orleans for a quick stop, then run, don't walk, to snag this sandwich. It's best topped with shredded lettuce, tomato, and dill pickle chips.

Makes: 2 loaded po' boys
Active time: 20 minutes
Total time: 1 hour 20 minutes

1 cup buttermilk

1 tablespoon hot sauce, such as Louisiana Brand

2 teaspoons salt, divided

½ teaspoon freshly ground black pepper

1 pound large shrimp, peeled and deveined

1 cup flour

¾ cup yellow cornmeal

½ teaspoon onion powder

½ teaspoon garlic powder

½ teaspoon cayenne pepper

¾ teaspoon paprika

2 quarts neutral oil (such as peanut or vegetable)

2 (8-inch) French bread rolls

1 large tomato, sliced

1 cup shredded lettuce

dill pickle slices

1. In a medium bowl, mix together the buttermilk, hot sauce, 1½ teaspoons salt, and pepper. Place the shrimp in the mixture and marinate in the refrigerator for 30 minutes to an hour.

2. In a medium bowl, mix the flour, cornmeal, onion powder, garlic powder, cayenne, paprika, and remaining ½ teaspoon salt. Shake the marinade from the chilled shrimp and place them in the flour mixture, turning to coat completely. Place the shrimp on a wire rack while you heat the oil for frying.

3. Pour the oil into a large pot, filling it about one-third to halfway, and heat over high heat until the oil reaches 350°F. (Clip a cooking thermometer to the side of the pot or dip it into the oil.) In batches, fry the shrimp in the oil for 2 to 3 minutes, until golden and cooked through. Drain on a plate lined with paper towels.

Did You Know?

In most countries, Ticket to Ride keeps its original name. But in certain markets the name has been translated, such as Zug um Zug in Germany or Les Aventuriers du Rail in France.

REMOULADE SAUCE

½ cup mayonnaise

¾ teaspoon paprika

1 teaspoon horseradish mustard

1 tablespoon finely chopped dill pickles

½ teaspoon cayenne pepper

½ teaspoon garlic powder

4. To make the remoulade sauce, in a small bowl combine the mayonnaise, paprika, mustard, chopped pickles, cayenne, and garlic powder.

5. Slice the rolls in half, lightly toast, and spread the remoulade sauce on both sides. Add lettuce, tomatoes, pickle slices, and shrimp to one half, then top with the other half to complete each sandwich.

DIRTY RICE

Getting its name from its "dirty" appearance after being cooked with meat, veggies, and spices, this Dirty Rice (or Cajun Rice) is a Louisiana Creole-style dish of rich meats, fluffy rice, and plenty of spice. This version includes the addition of chipotle for a smoky punch. This recipe uses ground beef and pork, but feel free to throw a wild card into the mix and use any of your favorite cuts.

Makes: 4 servings
Active time: 30 minutes
Total time: 40 minutes

4½ cups chicken broth, divided

2 cups uncooked long-grain white rice

2 bay leaves

1 pound ground beef (preferably 20 percent fat)

1 pound ground pork sausage

1 medium onion, chopped

1 celery rib, chopped

1 green bell pepper, chopped

1 tablespoon canned chipotles in adobo or chipotle hot sauce

3 cloves garlic, minced

1 tablespoon Cajun seasoning

2 tablespoons chopped fresh parsley

½ cup toasted and chopped pecans

zest of 1 lemon

salt and pepper, to taste

1. Add 3 cups of chicken broth to a large heavy pot over medium-high heat. Once it comes to a boil, add the rice and bay leaves. Stir gently to combine, letting the broth return to a boil and then immediately reducing the heat to medium-low. Cover the pot and simmer for 20 minutes, until the rice is tender. Remove from the heat and let rest for 5 minutes, then remove the bay leaves and use a fork to fluff the rice.

2. While the rice is cooking, brown the ground beef and pork sausage in a large skillet over medium heat, breaking up the meat with a fork. Work in batches to avoid crowding the pan. You want those brown crusty bits. Remove the meat to a bowl but leave the fat in the pan. Add the onion, celery, green pepper, and chipotles to the pan, cooking until the vegetables are tender, stirring occasionally, about 7 to 9 minutes.

3. Reduce the heat to low and add the garlic and Cajun seasoning, cooking for 1 minute while stirring constantly. Gently fold in the cooked rice, meat, and remaining 1½ cups chicken broth; cook for an additional 5 minutes. Stir in the parsley, pecans, and lemon zest, and season to taste with salt and pepper.

POSSUM PIE

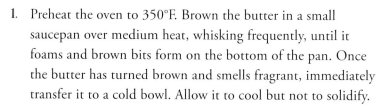

This Arkansas pie loads up a buttery shortbread crust with layers of sweet cream cheese and chocolate pudding, all crowned with whipped cream, shaved chocolate, and toasted pecans. This pie gets its name from the expression "to play possum," hinting at how the whipped cream hides the mysterious layers underneath.

Makes: 1 (9-inch) pie
Active time: 20 minutes
Total time: 4 hours 40 minutes

CRUST
½ cup (1 stick) unsalted butter
30 shortbread cookies
¾ cup toasted pecans
1 teaspoon kosher salt

CREAM CHEESE LAYER
6 ounces cream cheese, softened
½ cup powdered sugar
2 tablespoons heavy cream
zest of 1 lemon

PUDDING LAYER
1 (3.4-ounce) package chocolate pudding mix
2 cups cold whole milk
2 shots (2 ounces) cold espresso or rehydrated espresso powder
2 teaspoons vanilla extract
1 teaspoon kosher salt

TOPPING
½ cup heavy whipping cream
2 tablespoons powdered sugar
2 teaspoons vanilla extract
1 teaspoon kosher salt
1 to 2 tablespoons chopped, toasted pecans
2 tablespoons shaved dark chocolate

1. Preheat the oven to 350°F. Brown the butter in a small saucepan over medium heat, whisking frequently, until it foams and brown bits form on the bottom of the pan. Once the butter has turned brown and smells fragrant, immediately transfer it to a cold bowl. Allow it to cool but not to solidify.

2. Add the cookies, pecans, and salt to a food processor or blender. Pulse until everything is finely ground (about 15 pulses for a food processor). As you run the processor or blender, stream in the browned butter.

3. Press the mixture into the bottom of a 9-inch pie plate. Bake for 15 to 20 minutes, just until the crust begins to brown around the edges. Remove from the oven and let cool completely on a cooling rack.

4. For the cream cheese layer, in a medium bowl use a hand mixer (or use the bowl of an electric mixer fitted with a paddle attachment) to blend the cream cheese, ½ cup powdered sugar, 2 tablespoons heavy cream, and lemon zest until smooth. Spread over the bottom of the cooled pie crust.

5. Prepare the pudding layer by mixing the pudding mix, milk, espresso, 2 teaspoons vanilla, and 1 teaspoon salt in a medium bowl. Whisk until combined according to package directions.

6. Once the cream cheese layer is set, top it with the chocolate pudding. Cover with plastic wrap and refrigerate for 4 hours, until the pudding is set.

7. In a large bowl, use a hand mixer to whip together the ½ cup heavy cream, 2 tablespoons powdered sugar, 2 teaspoons vanilla, and 1 teaspoon salt until stiff peaks form. Spread the whipped cream over the top of the chocolate pudding layer. Sprinkle on the chopped pecans and chocolate shavings before slicing and serving the pie.

SAZERAC

The Sazerac may have been named the official cocktail of New Orleans in 2008, but this strong, kicky drink has been sipped since the 1800s. Peychaud's bitters and absinthe give it notes of black licorice (further emphasized by the five-spice glass rim), and the rest is all sweetness and whiskey that's as lively as the city it represents—and your game.

Makes: 2 drinks
Total time: 5 minutes

absinthe, for rinsing the glasses

Chinese five-spice powder, for glass rim

4 ounces (½ cup) simple syrup

3 ounces (6 tablespoons) rye whiskey

6 dashes Peychaud's bitters

4 dashes Angostura bitters

lemon twist, for garnish

1. Rinse two chilled coupe glasses with absinthe. Rim half of each glass in water and then the five-spice powder.

2. In a mixing glass filled with ice, stir the simple syrup, whiskey, and bitters until well chilled.

3. Strain the mixture into the glasses. Squeeze a lemon twist over each glass to extract the oils, then drop it into the glass.

> **Did You Know?**
> Throughout the years, 3 continents, more than 10 countries, and 6 cities around the world have received their own game board. But there is also a version where the board covers the entire world: Ticket to Ride Rails & Sails.

EAST

NEW ENGLAND CLAM CHOWDER

While Manhattanites may swear by a tomato-based chowder, classic New England chowder pairs sweet, briny clams with a velvety cream base. A finish of lemon zest cuts the richness for a balanced pregame slurp.

Makes: 4 servings
Active time: 30 minutes
Total time: 45 minutes

3 tablespoons unsalted butter

2 celery ribs, chopped

1 large onion, chopped

1 clove garlic, minced

3 small russet potatoes, peeled and cubed

1 cup water

1 (8-ounce) bottle clam juice

3 teaspoons chicken bouillon granules

¼ teaspoon pepper

¼ teaspoon dried thyme

4 cups peanut or canola oil

½ cup plus ⅓ cup flour, divided

2 tablespoons cornstarch

2 teaspoons kosher salt

1 leek

2 cups half-and-half, divided

2 (6½-ounce) cans chopped clams with brine

zest of 1 lemon

1. In a large Dutch oven over medium-high heat, melt the butter and sauté the celery and onion until tender. Add the garlic and cook 1 minute longer. Stir in the potatoes, water, clam juice, bouillon, pepper, and thyme. Bring to a boil, then reduce the heat to low and simmer, uncovered, until the potatoes are tender, 15 to 20 minutes.

2. While the potatoes are simmering, in a large pot over medium-high heat, preheat the oil to 350°F.

3. In a medium bowl, combine ½ cup flour with the cornstarch and salt. Cut the leek into slices as thin as possible (a mandolin makes this easy), through the beginning of the green tops. Using your hands, toss in the flour mixture.

4. Working in batches to avoid overcrowding, fry the leek slices in the hot oil for 30 to 60 seconds, until lightly browned. Strain and transfer to a paper-towel-lined baking sheet.

5. In a small bowl, combine the ⅓ cup flour and 1 cup half-and-half until smooth. Gradually stir the mixture into the soup. Raise to medium-high heat and bring to a boil. Cook until thickened, stirring for 1 to 2 minutes. Stir in the clams and remaining 1 cup of half-and-half; heat through but do not boil.

6. Ladle the soup into bowls to serve, topping each serving with fried leek slices and lemon zest.

LOBSTER ROLL

What do first-class train riders do for lunch in the fall? They indulge in the ultimate New England sweet-and-salty seafood treat—the lobster roll—during its peak season. This simple sandwich relies on quality shellfish; a toasted, buttery bun; and a rich, creamy combo of butter and mayonnaise. Make sure to grab extra napkins to spare your white linen tablecloth!

Makes: 4 rolls
Active time: 35 minutes
Total time: 35 minutes

1 pound frozen lobster meat, thawed, or cooked meat from two 1½- to 2-pound fresh lobsters

¼ cup minced celery

¼ cup mayonnaise

1 tablespoon minced chives, plus more for garnish

1 tablespoon chopped fresh tarragon

1 tablespoon lemon juice

1 teaspoon lemon zest

¼ teaspoon kosher salt, or to taste

¼ teaspoon freshly ground pepper, or to taste

4 tablespoons (½ stick) unsalted butter, divided

4 New England–style top-split brioche hot dog buns

1. Rinse and pick through the lobster meat to remove any loose shells. Drain thoroughly. Chop or tear into large chunks and set aside.

2. In a large bowl, mix the celery, mayonnaise, chives, tarragon, lemon juice and zest, salt, and pepper. Taste for seasoning and adjust as needed.

3. In a large skillet over medium heat, melt 2 tablespoons of butter and add the lobster meat. Cook, stirring, for 2 minutes, until warmed through and buttery all over. Use a slotted spoon to transfer the lobster meat into the mayonnaise mixture; toss to coat.

4. Wipe out the skillet, discarding the pan butter and juice released from the lobster. Melt the remaining 2 tablespoons butter in the skillet over medium heat. Add the buns and toast for about 2 minutes on each side until golden and toasty.

5. Load the buns equally with the lobster meat and garnish with more chives, if desired.

CHARRED SUCCOTASH WITH ELOTE CREMA

Succotash is derived from a Narragansett Indian word, msickquatash—a simmering pot of corn. The Narragansett are native to what is now Rhode Island, and they used whatever fresh, seasonal produce was available. Nowadays, you'll find succotash on Thanksgiving tables throughout New England. This version holds true to the classic while also drawing inspiration from the rich and creamy spiciness of Mexican street corn.

Makes: 4 servings
Active time: 45 minutes
Total time: 45 minutes

ELOTE SAUCE

1 canned chipotle pepper in adobo sauce

2 cloves garlic

10 stalks cilantro

zest and juice of 1 lime

1 cup Mexican crema or sour cream

1 cup southern mayonnaise (such as Duke's)

½ cup cotija cheese, crumbled

SUCCOTASH

2 cups frozen lima beans

6 center-cut bacon slices

1 cup frozen pearl onions

1 cup fresh okra, cut in ½-inch-thick slices

3 cups fresh corn kernels (approximately 4 ears)

1¼ teaspoons kosher salt

¼ teaspoon black pepper

3 tablespoons unsalted butter

2 cloves garlic

1 cup (5 ounces) cherry tomatoes, halved

1. To make the elote sauce, finely chop the chipotle pepper and garlic. Cut off the cilantro leaves, roughly chop them, and set aside. Mince the cilantro stalks and place in a mixing bowl along with the chipotle and garlic. Add the lime zest and juice, crema or sour cream, and mayonnaise, then stir in the cotija cheese. Set aside to allow the flavors to develop.

2. In a medium saucepan, add the lima beans and cover with water. Simmer on high heat until cooked, about 3 minutes. While the beans simmer, place the bacon slices in a large cast-iron skillet over medium heat. Cook until crisp, about 8 minutes, turning after 5 minutes. Transfer the bacon to paper towels, crumble into small pieces, and set aside. Reserve the skillet drippings.

3. In the skillet used for the bacon, cook the pearl onions and okra slices over medium heat until just tender and slightly browned, about 6 to 8 minutes. Then stir in the corn kernels, salt, pepper, and drained lima beans. Cook, stirring often, until the corn is tender and bright yellow, 7 to 9 minutes. Finely mince the garlic and add it to the skillet along with the butter. Cook, stirring constantly, until the butter is melted and the garlic is fragrant, about a minute. Remove from the heat.

4. To serve, stir in the bacon and halved cherry tomatoes then top with the chilled elote sauce.

BOSTON CREAM PIE

Want to sweeten up the game? This classic cake gets a regional update by adding cranberry flavoring to the cream filling and then covering the whole thing with a bitter chocolate glaze. And just why is this cake, popularized at a Boston hotel in the nineteenth century, called a pie? Back then, pie tins were more readily available than cake pans for baking, and the pie moniker stuck.

Makes: 1 (9-inch, 2-layer) cake
Active time: 45 minutes
Total time: 1 hour 45 minutes

2½ cups sugar, divided

4 large eggs plus 4 large egg yolks, divided

⅓ cup vegetable oil

2⅓ cups flour, divided

4 teaspoons salt, divided

2 teaspoons baking powder

4 tablespoons (½ stick) butter, at room temperature

2½ cups whole milk, divided

4 tablespoons vanilla extract, divided

1 cup cranberry juice cocktail

⅓ cup dark chocolate chips or chopped dark chocolate

¼ cup heavy cream or whipping cream

1 teaspoon espresso powder

2 tablespoons flaky sea salt

1. To make the cakes, preheat the oven to 325°F. Lightly grease two 9-inch round pans and line with parchment paper.

2. Using an electric mixer, beat 2 cups sugar and 4 eggs together until light and fluffy, about 2 minutes at medium-high speed. Continuing to beat, slowly drizzle in the vegetable oil.

3. Add 2 cups flour, 2 teaspoons salt, and the baking powder, beating with a whisk until just combined. Scrape the bottom and sides of the bowl, then beat again by hand, being careful not to overmix.

4. In a small saucepan over medium heat, bring the butter and 1 cup milk just to a boil. Remove from the heat and stir until the butter is completely melted, then stir in 2 tablespoons vanilla. Slowly add the hot milk mixture to the cake batter, mixing by hand until everything is well combined. Scrape the bowl and mix briefly, just until smooth. The batter will be very thin.

5. Divide the batter evenly between the pans. Bake for 30 to 35 minutes, until a toothpick inserted in the center comes out clean and the top feels set. Remove from the oven, let cool in the pans for 10 minutes, and then turn out onto a rack to cool completely.

6. To make the filling, in a medium saucepan bring the cranberry juice to a boil over medium-high heat. Boil, uncovered, until reduced by two-thirds, stirring constantly, about 6 to 8 minutes. Remove from the heat and let cool for a minute, then slowly add in ½ cup milk, ½ cup sugar, and 2 teaspoons salt. Return to the stovetop over medium heat and whisk constantly until the mixture just begins to simmer.

7. In a medium bowl, whisk the remaining ⅓ cup flour and egg yolks with the remaining 1cup milk until smooth. Very slowly whisk in about half of the simmering cranberry mixture. Then pour into the pan with remaining simmering cranberry/milk mixture and whisk to combine.

8. Pour the mixture into a bowl through a fine mesh strainer and then pour the strained mixture back into the pan. Bring to a low boil over medium heat, stirring constantly with a whisk, and cook for 2 minutes; the mixture will thicken significantly. Remove from the heat and stir in 1 tablespoon vanilla. Transfer the filling to a heatproof bowl and top with a piece of buttered plastic wrap to prevent a skin from forming. Refrigerate until cool.

9. When the cake layers and pastry cream are completely cool, set one layer on a serving plate and spread the filling evenly over the top, and then add the second layer. Set aside.

10. To make the glaze, use a microwave set at 50 percent power to heat the chocolate, cream, and espresso powder in a microwave-safe bowl for 1 to 3 minutes until melted, stirring every 30 seconds. Add 1 tablespoon vanilla and stir well. Let sit for about 10 minutes to cool and thicken, then pour over the filled cake and sprinkle with the sea salt. Serve immediately or, once cooled, store in an airtight container for 2 to 3 days.

NEW ENGLAND CIDER

Humble cider is transformed here into a layered, complex drink that'll thaw you out during even the coldest New England winter. And while the state of Washington might grow 60 percent of America's apples, New York is right behind them in bushels. Toasted cinnamon, ginger, cloves, and other warming spices add depth to this cider, which is excellent either with or without whiskey. Brew it up on a cold winter night for your group of gamers.

Makes: 4 servings
Active time: 15 minutes
Total time: 35 minutes

4 tablespoons whiskey (optional)

¼ cup sherry vinegar

¼ cup honey

2 tablespoons blackstrap molasses

8 cups (2 quarts) apple cider

10 dashes orange bitters

sliced oranges, for garnish

SPICE MIX
1 tablespoon ground cinnamon

½ tablespoon ground ginger

1 teaspoon ground cloves

1 teaspoon freshly ground nutmeg

1 tablespoon smoked paprika

1. In a large, heavy-bottomed pot over medium heat, stir together all the spices for the spice mix and toast until fragrant, about 2 minutes.

2. Add the whiskey, if using, and cook until it is reduced by half, burning off some of the alcohol. Add the sherry vinegar, honey, and molasses and cook for 1 minute. Reduce the heat to medium-low, add the cider, and simmer for 20 minutes. (But if you have more time, it will only get better!)

3. Ladle the cider into mugs and add 2 dashes of bitters to each serving. Garnish with sliced oranges—and you can always spike it with extra whiskey.

HALF-SMOKE SAUSAGE BITES

An icon of cuisine in Washington, DC, half-smoke sausages are a regionally unique take on the hot dog. If you don't have a Destination Ticket that routes you through DC to pick up these spicier, more coarsely ground sausages, you can also substitute any cased, smoked sausage to make these little bites. Pair with pickled onions and deli mustard, or simply grab and go.

Makes: 4 servings
Active time: 30 minutes
Total time: 1 hour

1 sheet frozen puff pastry

1 large onion

3 tablespoons apple cider vinegar

1 teaspoon salt

8 ounces smoked sausages (see note)

1 egg, beaten

3 tablespoons sesame seeds or everything bagel seasoning

½ cup deli mustard

2 teaspoons crushed red pepper flakes (optional)

1. Defrost the puffed pastry in the refrigerator according to the package directions, then cut into strips the length of a sausage, wide enough to roll around the sausage.

2. To pickle the onion, slice it paper-thin and add to a bowl with the vinegar and salt. Let sit for at least 45 minutes.

3. Preheat the oven to 425°F. Sear the sausages in a large pan on the stovetop over medium-high heat until browned on the outside, 5 to 7 minutes. Remove and let cool.

4. Place a whole sausage on a piece of puffed pastry. Roll it up so that the pastry covers the sides of the sausage. The ends will stick out. Repeat for the remaining sausages, then place the rolls on a baking sheet and brush with the beaten egg. Sprinkle the tops with sesame seeds or everything bagel seasoning.

5. Cook in the oven until the puffed pastry is golden brown and crisp, about 12 to 15 minutes. Remove and let rest for 5 minutes.

6. Slice into ½-inch rounds and plate with the pickled onions, mustard, and—for extra heat—sprinkle with crushed red pepper flakes.

Note
Half-smokes are ubiquitous in DC; even the Washington Nationals baseball team has deemed them their "official dog." Despite this, they are harder to find once you've left the city limits. It's worth the online trip (and the shipping) to get the real thing!

NEW YORK-STYLE PIZZA

Have you drawn a Destination Ticket that routes you through New York City? You're in luck. Foldable slices of melty mozzarella and giant pepperoni pizza will greet you at this well-connected station. But pizza perfection doesn't happen quickly. Plan ahead and let the dough rest for at least 24 hours before stretching and baking it. The resulting crisp, chewy crust will be worth the wait.

Makes: 2 (12-inch) pizzas
Active time: 30 minutes
Total time: 27 hours 15 minutes

CRUST
1 cup plus 1 tablespoon cold water (add more as needed)

3 cups bread flour

1 teaspoon instant dry yeast

1½ teaspoons salt

1 teaspoon sugar

1 tablespoon olive oil

SAUCE
1 tablespoon olive oil

1 tablespoon unsalted butter

3 cloves garlic, crushed

1 teaspoon dried oregano

1 (28-ounce) can crushed tomatoes

1 teaspoon onion powder

1 teaspoon sugar

½ teaspoon salt

TOPPINGS
2 cups grated full-fat mozzarella cheese

pepperoni slices

SPECIAL EQUIPMENT
pizza stone

stand mixer with a dough hook

1. To make the crust, pour water into the bowl of the stand mixer. In a separate medium bowl, mix the flour, yeast, 1½ teaspoons salt, and 1 teaspoon sugar. Using the dough hook attachment, gradually add the flour mixture to the water. (If it's too dry, add more water a teaspoon at a time). Once the flour is just incorporated, add the oil and knead for 8 minutes with the mixer at medium-high speed.

2. Divide the dough into two balls, place in separate large ziplock bags, and put in the refrigerator for at least 24 hours or up to three days.

3. About 2 hours before you're ready to bake, remove the dough from the refrigerator and let it come to room temperature. An hour before baking, set your pizza stone in the oven and preheat the oven to 550°F.

4. Meanwhile, make the sauce. In a medium saucepan over medium-low heat, combine the olive oil and butter. Heat until the butter is just melted, then add the garlic and oregano and cook for 1 to 2 minutes. Add the crushed tomatoes, onion powder, 1 teaspoon sugar, and ½ teaspoon salt and bring to a simmer. Then turn the heat down to low and cook uncovered for 45 minutes, stirring occasionally.

5. Spread parchment paper onto a flat surface, add the dough, and gently stretch it to your desired size. Top with sauce, cheese, pepperoni slices, and any other desired toppings. Slide the pizza onto the pizza stone (including the parchment paper is okay) and bake for 6 to 8 minutes, until the cheese is just starting to brown. When done, remove from the oven and allow to rest for 2 to 3 minutes before slicing and serving.

GARLIC KNOTS WITH CALABRIAN CHILE SAUCE

Put leftover pizza dough to good use with this tasty appetizer—though these little nuggets are worthy of their own dough-making session, too. Garlic knots are perfect for grabbing and munching on while riding the rails, and these pack a punch with a spicy Calabrian chile–laced marinara sauce.

Makes: 4 servings
Active time: 1 hour
Total time: 3 hours

⅔ cup warm water (100° to 110°F)

1 (¼-ounce) packet active dry yeast (2¼ teaspoons)

2 tablespoons olive oil, plus more for brushing

2 teaspoons sugar

1¼ teaspoons kosher salt, divided

1¾ cups bread flour (or as needed), plus more for dusting

1 small bunch fresh parsley, divided

4 tablespoons (½ stick) unsalted butter

6 cloves garlic, minced

2 tablespoons grated parmesan cheese, plus more for sprinkling

2 cups marinara sauce

1 tablespoon chopped jarred Calabrian chiles

1. Place the warm water in a large bowl and sprinkle with the active dry yeast. Let sit for 5 to 10 minutes to activate and then add the 2 tablespoons olive oil, sugar, and 1 teaspoon salt; whisk to combine.

2. Add the 1¾ cups flour and stir with a wooden spoon until a sticky, uniform dough forms. Cover the bowl with a tea towel or plastic wrap and let rise in a warm spot until doubled in size, about an hour.

3. Line two baking sheets with parchment paper and lightly flour a work surface. Transfer the dough onto the work surface and knead five to ten times to bring it together into a smooth ball. Cut the dough into 12 pieces.

4. Working with a single piece at a time, use your hands to roll the dough into an even 8-inch rope about ½ inch thick; if needed, add just enough flour to keep the dough from sticking. Tie into a knot. Arrange the dough knots on the baking sheets, spacing them evenly. Cover loosely with a tea towel and let rest until the dough puffs slightly, about 15 minutes. When you press a finger into the dough, it should bounce back slowly.

5. While the dough is rising, arrange two oven racks to divide the oven into thirds. Preheat the oven to 425°F. Finely chop the parsley leaves until you have 4 tablespoons.

6. Heat the butter in a small saucepan over medium heat until just melted. Remove the saucepan from the heat. Add the garlic, 3 tablespoons parsley, parmesan cheese, and remaining ¼ teaspoon salt, stirring to combine. Uncover the dough and generously brush the knots with the butter mixture, using all of it. Then bake until just cooked through and golden brown, 15 to 19 minutes.

7. While the knots are baking, warm the marinara sauce in a small saucepan over medium-low heat. Add the Calabrian chiles and cook for at least 10 minutes, stirring occasionally.

8. Brush the baked knots with more olive oil and sprinkle with the remaining tablespoon of parsley and more grated parmesan. Serve with the sauce.

New York Cheesecake with Cherry Sauce

The only thing richer than a railroad tycoon is this cheesecake. This is an intensely creamy cake, with a lightly spiced crust made of speculoos cookies, a tangy filling that blends cream and goat cheeses, and a luxurious cherry sauce tinged with the flavors of a classic Manhattan cocktail (page 45).

Makes: 8 servings
Active time: 1 hour
Total time: 12 hours

CRUST

1 cup (2 sticks) unsalted butter, or more as needed

12 ounces speculoos cookies

1 cup walnuts, toasted

¼ cup dark brown sugar

2 teaspoons salt

¼ cup flour

FILLING

4 (8-ounce) blocks cream cheese, at room temperature

8 ounces goat cheese, at room temperature

1 cup granulated sugar

2 teaspoons salt

¼ cup cornstarch

½ cup Mexican crema or sour cream

zest of 1 lemon

1 tablespoon vanilla extract

5 large eggs plus 2 yolks

1. Brown the butter in a small saucepan over medium heat, whisking frequently until it foams and brown bits form on the bottom of the pan. When the butter is brown and smells fragrant, immediately put it into a cold bowl to keep it from cooking any further. Allow it to cool but not to solidify.

2. Preheat the oven to 350°F. Add the cookies, walnuts, brown sugar, salt, and flour to a food processor or a blender and spin until broken into a sandy texture. Drizzle in the butter 1 tablespoon at a time while spinning until the mixture just begins to hold together when pinched. If it's still crumbly, spin in a bit more butter.

3. Grease a 9-inch springform pan, then press half the cookie mixture evenly against the pan sides. Press the remaining crumbs into an even layer on the bottom of the pan.

4. Bake for 10 minutes and then transfer to the refrigerator to cool. Reduce the oven temperature to 325°F.

5. Place the cream cheese, goat cheese, sugar, salt, and cornstarch in the bowl of a stand mixer fitted with the paddle attachment (if you don't have a stand mixer, you can use an electric mixer or a sturdy whisk). Mix on medium speed, scraping the sides of the bowl after about 30 seconds. Mix for another minute or so until well combined. Add in the sour cream, lemon zest, and vanilla and continue to mix for another minute until the ingredients are combined. Scrape the mixer paddle and bowl well. Then, with the mixer on medium speed, add the eggs and yolks one at a time, mixing until just combined and scraping the sides of the bowl halfway through, being careful not to overmix.

MANHATTAN SAUCE

12 ounces frozen cherries

1 teaspoon salt

⅔ cup dark brown sugar

zest and juice of 1 lemon

2 tablespoons rye whiskey

1 tablespoon cornstarch

8 dashes Angostura bitters

SPECIAL EQUIPMENT

9-inch springform pan

6. Pour the mixture into the cooled crust and bake at 325°F for 1 hour. The cheesecake should still be jiggly in the center. Turn the oven off and let the cheesecake cool in the oven with the door closed for 45 minutes. Then remove from the oven and let come to room temperature. Tent with foil and refrigerate for at least 10 hours.

7. To make the Manhattan sauce, add the cherries, 1 teaspoon salt, ¾ cup brown sugar, and the lemon zest and juice to a sauté pan over high heat. In a separate bowl, create a slurry by whisking the whiskey and cornstarch together. Add to the pan just as the mixture begins to boil, reduce to medium heat, and cook down for 5 to 6 minutes. Stir in the bitters, remove from the heat, and transfer to a bowl to cool. Refrigerate until ready to use for topping your cheesecake. To serve, remove refrigerated cheesecake, place on a cake stand, and top with cherry sauce. Dip a chef's knife in hot tap water and cut into slices. Drizzle slices with additional sauce.

Did You Know?

Ticket to Ride has an expansion pack! Ticket to Ride – USA 1910 uses the same game board but has a new game deck, destination tickets, a Globe Trotter card for completing the most tickets, and more fun ways to take the base game to the next level.

Manhattan

There may be no better drink to sip while boasting about your burgeoning rail empire than the classic Manhattan. One of the most sophisticated cocktails around, the Manhattan is smooth and complex, a favorite of fancy drinkers across the continent. While its history is a bit murky (some legends say it was named for the Manhattan Club, where it was served in the 1880s), its status as a cocktail icon is undisputed.

Makes: 2 drinks
Total time: 5 minutes

4 ounces (½ cup) rye whiskey
2 ounces (¼ cup) sweet vermouth
4 dashes Angostura bitters
Luxardo maraschino cherries and/
or lemon twists, for garnish

1. In a mixing glass filled with ice, stir together the rye whiskey, vermouth, and bitters until well chilled.

2. Spoon a Luxardo cherry with a bit of its syrup into the base of two chilled cocktail glasses. Strain the drink into the glasses and garnish each with more cherries and/or a lemon twist.

COLLARD GREENS

Any true Southerner knows that the best part of collard greens is the pot likker—the liquid left behind after slow-simmering the greens. This sublime broth is a savory melding of all the porky goodness of bacon and andouille sausage combined with stock, seasoning, and a little bitterness from the greens. This is the perfect first course dish for an overnight train journey—the warm and hearty broth paired with the gentle rock of the sleeper car guarantees a good night's sleep.

Makes: 6 servings
Active time: 20 minutes
Total time: 2 hours 20 minutes

12 thick-cut bacon slices

1 pound andouille sausage, chopped into small pieces

2 yellow onions, finely chopped

6 cloves garlic, diced

⅓ cup plus 2 tablespoons red wine vinegar, divided

64 ounces (2 quarts) chicken broth

3 pounds fresh collard greens, trimmed

1 tablespoon sugar

1 teaspoon kosher salt

1 teaspoon black pepper

2 teaspoons crushed red pepper flakes

zest of 1 lemon

1. Cook the bacon in a large stockpot over medium heat for 10 to 12 minutes, until crisp, then remove and crumble it into a small bowl.

2. In the same pot, cook the andouille sausage cubes in the bacon fat until slightly brown, about 5 to 7 minutes. Remove and add to the bowl with the bacon. Remove all but 3 tablespoons of the pork fat from the pot.

3. Add the onion to the stockpot and sauté for 8 minutes, stirring occasionally.

4. Add the garlic and sauté until fragrant, about 1 minute. Pour in ⅓ cup of vinegar to deglaze the bottom of the pot.

5. Stir in the broth, collard greens, sugar, salt, black pepper, and red pepper flakes. Reduce to medium-low heat and cook, covered, for 2 hours, or until your desired degree of tenderness is achieved.

6. Finish by returning the bacon and sausage to the pot and adding an additional 2 tablespoons vinegar for the last 5 minutes of cooking. Dish up the greens with plenty of the pot likker and top with lemon zest.

CUBANO

In 1900, the first recorded mention of the Cubano sandwich came from Florida, where many Cuban immigrants worked in cigar factories. The combo of pork, ham, melted Swiss cheese, and sharp mustard and pickles is made even better with sweet, pillowy-soft bread. This sandwich is a must whenever your travels take you through the Sunshine State.

Makes: 4 servings
Active time: 10 minutes
Total time: 30 minutes

1 pound cooked pork butt roast, shredded

3 tablespoons butter, melted

3 cloves garlic, minced

1 loaf Cuban or French bread

¼ cup yellow mustard

10 slices swiss cheese

10 slices deli ham

10 to 15 dill pickle slices

potato chips, for serving

1. Preheat two large cast-iron skillets, nested one on top of the another, over medium heat; let them heat through. Alternatively, preheat a panini press to medium temperature. Place shredded pork on a baking pan and heat in a 250°F oven until warmed through, about 15 minutes.

2. Mix the melted butter and garlic in a small bowl. Slice the loaf of bread in half lengthwise and toast, cut side down, in your dry skillets or panini press until golden brown. You may need to slice the loaf into pieces to fit in your pans.

3. Remove the toasted bread. On one half of the loaf, spread the garlic butter. On the other half, generously spread the mustard. Layer the Swiss cheese, warmed pork, ham, and sliced pickles on one half and then top with the second half.

4. Add the sandwiches to the first skillet and cover with the second preheated skillet, pushing down. Grill for 5 to 6 minutes per side. If you're using a panini press, grill for 6 minutes total, or until the cheese is melted and the top of the bread is crispy and brown. Cut into four sandwiches and serve with potato chips.

PLANTAIN CHIPS

Cuban cuisine has significantly influenced that of Florida, and plantain chips are one of the quintessential starchy staples highlighting that connection. Crispy on the outside but still tender on the inside, this snack gets some zip from chipotle powder and lime zest. It's perfect by the handful around the game table.

Makes: 4 servings
Active time: 20 minutes
Total time: 20 minutes

2 tablespoons salt
1 tablespoon pepper
1 tablespoon chipotle powder
zest of 1 lime
2 quarts peanut oil
4 large, green plantains

1. To make the spice blend, in a small bowl combine the salt, pepper, chipotle powder, and lime zest.

2. In a large, heavy-bottomed pot over medium-high, heat the oil to 375°F. Using a sharp knife, remove the hard peel of the plantains and slice them into ⅛-inch rounds (a mandolin makes this easy). Place the sliced plantains on a baking sheet lined with paper towels, and use additional paper towels to pat them dry.

3. Working in batches, fry the plantain slices in the oil until they are golden brown, about 1 minute. Remove from the oil with a spider strainer or slotted spoon and place on a paper towel–lined baking sheet. Immediately sprinkle with the seasoning mixture. Transfer to a serving bowl and serve hot.

Did You Know?

Ever since its birth in 2004, Ticket to Ride can be seen throughout pop culture. You'll notice it in many television series, such as *The Big Bang Theory* or *The IT Crowd*.

COCONUT CAKE

In the South, a celebration without coconut cake just isn't a celebration. The luscious white cake wrapped in cream cheese frosting and sweetened shredded coconut is the centerpiece of every gathering, which makes it the perfect reward after you've completed all your Destination Tickets. Even better? This version of the tropical cake reveals a surprise inside—zesty lime curd.

> Makes: 1 (9-inch, 2-layer) cake
> Active time: 10 minutes
> Total time: 1 hour

CURD

1 cup sugar

3 large eggs, at room temperature

1 cup fresh lime juice, approximately 8 limes

zest of 5 limes

½ cup (1 stick) unsalted butter, melted

CAKE

1½ cups (3 sticks) unsalted butter, at room temperature, plus more for greasing pans

2 cups sugar

5 large eggs, at room temperature

2 teaspoons vanilla extract

1 teaspoon coconut extract

3 cups flour, plus more for dusting the pans

1 teaspoon baking powder

½ teaspoon baking soda

1 teaspoon kosher salt

1 cup whole milk

1 cup shredded unsweetened coconut

1. To make the curd, in a large, microwave-safe bowl whisk together the sugar, eggs, lime juice, lime zest, and melted butter. Place the bowl in the microwave and cook on full power in 1-minute intervals. Stir well after each minute, for 3 to 5 minutes total. The curd should become thick enough to coat the back of a spoon. Pass it through a fine sieve to remove any lumps, then refrigerate.

2. To make the cake, preheat the oven to 350°F. Grease two 9-inch round cake pans and line with parchment paper. Grease the parchment paper and dust lightly with flour.

3. In the bowl of an electric mixer fitted with the paddle attachment, cream the butter and sugar on medium-high speed for 3 to 5 minutes, until pale and fluffy. With the mixer on medium speed, add the eggs one at a time and then the extracts, scraping down the sides of the bowl once during mixing.

4. In a separate bowl, sift together the flour, baking powder, baking soda, and salt. Then, with the mixer on low speed, alternately add the dry ingredients and the milk to the batter in thirds, beginning and ending with the dry ingredients. Mix until just combined, then mix in the shredded coconut until just combined.

5. Pour the batter evenly into the two pans and bake in the center of the oven for 45 to 55 minutes, until the tops are browned and a cake tester comes out clean. Cool on a baking rack for 30 minutes, then turn out of the pans onto the rack to cool completely.

FROSTING

1 pound (2 blocks) cream cheese, at room temperature

½ pound (2 sticks) unsalted butter, at room temperature

2 teaspoons vanilla extract

1 teaspoon coconut extract

3 cups powdered sugar

6 ounces or 2 cups sweetened shredded coconut

lime zest, for garnish (optional)

6. For the frosting, use the electric mixer on low speed to combine the cream cheese, butter, vanilla, and coconut extract. Add the powdered sugar and mix until smooth.

7. To assemble the cake, place one layer on a flat serving plate, top side down, and spread with frosting. Spoon the lime curd into the center of the cake over the frosting, then spread to within an inch of the edge.

8. Place the second layer on top, flat side down. Frost the top and sides of the cake with the remaining frosting. Sprinkle shredded coconut on top and press more into the sides. If desired, sprinkle with lime zest. To store, wrap in plastic wrap and/or place in an airtight container and refrigerate.

Did You Know?

Ticket to Ride is also a video game success story. With a first version in 2005, Ticket to Ride has always expanded to as many video game platforms as possible, with an all-new version released at the end of 2023.

MOJITO

It didn't take long for the mojito to make its way from its birthplace in Havana, Cuba, to south Florida. This drink is far too delicious to stay in any one place! The sweet, tangy blend of lime, mint, sugar, and rum is iconic, and this version kicks it up a notch with fresh-made mint simple syrup. Enjoy as a pregame cocktail before a hot night out on the town or as a cooling nightcap after a long evening of route building.

Makes: 2 drinks
Active time: 5 minutes
Total time: 35 minutes

1 cup sugar

1 cup water

1 cup fresh mint leaves, divided

4 ounces (½ cup) white rum

2 ounces (¼ cup) lime juice, plus lime slices, for garnish

1 cup club soda or sparkling water, as needed

1. To make the mint simple syrup, pour the sugar and water into a small saucepan; add ½ cup of the mint leaves. Bring to a boil over medium heat, stirring to dissolve the sugar. Simmer for 1 to 2 minutes, then remove from the heat and let sit for 20 to 30 minutes. Pour through a fine mesh strainer or scoop out the mint leaves.

2. Muddle a handful of the remaining mint leaves in the bottom of a cocktail shaker. Add the rum, lime juice, 1½ ounces of your mint simple syrup, and a few cubes of ice. Shake and then strain into two tall glasses filled with ice. Top with club soda or sparkling water and garnish with lime slices and more mint.

MIDWEST

MINNESOTA WILD RICE SOUP

Minnesota's state grain—yes, there is such a thing—is wild rice, a staple for the Ojibwe tribe for centuries. Since it's harvested from lakes, its heartiness holds up in soups such as this one, making for creamy slurping as you wind your way across the country. To make this dish vegan, you can use coconut milk instead of heavy cream.

Makes: 4 servings
Active time: 20 minutes
Total time: 50 minutes

1 cup uncooked wild rice

2 tablespoons unsalted butter

2 celery ribs, chopped

½ medium yellow onion, chopped

2 large carrots, peeled and chopped

4 cloves garlic, minced

1 teaspoon chopped fresh thyme, stem removed

1 bay leaf

5 cups chicken or vegetable broth

½ cup white wine

⅓ cup heavy cream

salt, to taste

olive oil, for drizzling

1. Cook the rice according to the package directions; wild rice typically takes 45 to 50 minutes to cook.

2. In a large pot over medium heat, melt the butter and add the celery, onion, and carrots. Cook for 4 to 5 minutes, or until just soft.

3. Add the garlic, thyme, and bay leaf and cook for 1 to 2 minutes more.

4. Pour in the broth and wine, turn up the heat to high, and bring to a boil. Then reduce the heat to low and let simmer for 10 minutes. Turn off the heat and stir in the cooked rice, heavy cream, and salt. To serve, ladle into bowls and drizzle a little olive oil into each bowl.

Did You Know?
Originally, the Switzerland board was only available on PC. Because of the growing demand within the community, Days of Wonder decided to create a physical expansion, which had a board that was specifically designed for two and three players.

Tomahawk Steak

Steak's importance to the Midwest goes beyond the region's meat-and-potatoes reputation—beef processing has been a key industry in Omaha, Kansas City, Chicago, and beyond. One of the steaks most worthy of game night is the tomahawk, a gloriously marbled, rib-bone-in, full-on meaty experience. With a simple topping of garlic rosemary butter, this steak gets to speak for itself.

Makes: 2 to 4 servings
Active time: 15 minutes
Total time: 13 hours 30 minutes

1 tomahawk steak, about 3 pounds

coarse kosher salt

pepper

3 sprigs fresh rosemary

3 cloves garlic

6 tablespoons unsalted butter, softened

1. Liberally salt the steak and place on a wire rack over a baking sheet. Refrigerate, uncovered, overnight.

2. Pat the steak dry with a paper towel and sprinkle it with pepper. Preheat the oven to 200°F.

3. Place a large skillet upside down over a burner set on high heat. (The bone can hinder getting a good sear on the steak so cooking on the back of the skillet allows the meat to make full contact with the pan surface.) Add the rosemary, garlic cloves, and steak to the pan surface. Sear for 2 minutes per side, then grab the steak by the bone and quickly sear the edges.

4. Place the steak on a rimmed baking sheet and bake until the internal temperature reaches 130°F. (Cooking times will vary, but start checking at around 40 minutes.)

5. While the steak is cooking, finely mince the seared garlic and rosemary and mix into the softened butter. Spread the mixture into flat 1-inch rounds on parchment paper and refrigerate to harden slightly.

6. When the steak is done, let it rest for 10 to 15 minutes before slicing across the grain in thin pieces. Place butter rounds on top of the slices to serve.

Cheesy Corn

Cheesy corn is in any good Midwestern route-builder's DNA, and really, what's not to like? The Kansas City BBQ staple combines cream cheese, cheddar, butter, corn, and sometimes bacon or ham in an ultra-rich, comforting bite. This recipe uses thick-cut bacon, but you can easily make this vegetarian by skipping the bacon.

Makes: 8 servings
Active time: 15 minutes
Total time: 30 minutes

1 tablespoon olive oil

1 tablespoon minced garlic

3 cups corn kernels, preferably roasted, but canned or frozen is fine

4 ounces cream cheese

2 tablespoons unsalted butter

¾ cup whole milk

1 teaspoon kosher salt

½ teaspoon black pepper

¼ teaspoon cayenne pepper

½ teaspoon paprika

1½ cups shredded cheddar cheese, divided

4 slices cooked, chopped thick-cut bacon, divided

¼ cup sliced green onions

1. Preheat the oven to 350°F. In a large skillet, heat the oil over medium heat and cook the garlic for 1 to 2 minutes.

2. Stir in the corn, cream cheese, butter, and milk. Reduce the heat to medium-low and cook until the ingredients are melted together, stirring occasionally, 5 to 7 minutes.

3. Stir in the salt, pepper, cayenne, paprika, ¾ cup of the shredded cheddar, and half the bacon. Pour into an 8 x 8-inch baking dish and sprinkle ¾ cup cheddar over the top.

4. Bake for 15 minutes, or until the top is golden. To serve, garnish with the green onions and the rest of the bacon.

Did You Know?

The online version of Ticket to Ride has led to some beautiful encounters. Days of Wonder has received numerous messages of heartfelt gratitude, and even wedding invitations from couples who met each other in game!

PECAN PIE

Pecan pie is a distinctly American creation, with the majority of the world's pecans grown in the US. In the late nineteenth century, someone thought to toast and douse the nuts in butter and sugar and bake them up in a crust, resulting in one of the first recipes for pecan pie, appearing in a St. Louis church charity cookbook. This gooey, crunchy pie has all the custardy richness you crave, with a hint of spice.

Makes: 1 (9-inch) pie
Active time: 50 minutes
Total time: 3 hours 20 minutes

CRUST

1¼ cups unbleached flour, chilled

1 tablespoon sugar

1 teaspoon salt

8 tablespoons (1 stick) cold unsalted butter, cubed, plus more for greasing the pan

1 large egg, lightly beaten

cold water, as needed

FILLING

1 cup light brown sugar, packed

3 tablespoons unsalted butter, melted

½ cup maple syrup

3 large eggs, beaten

2 cups pecans, chopped and lightly toasted

2 teaspoons vanilla extract

pinch of salt

2 teaspoons finely grated fresh ginger

EGG WASH

1 egg

1 tablespoon water

1. To make the crust, in a medium bowl whisk together the flour, 1 tablespoon sugar, and 1 teaspoon salt. Cut the stick of butter into the mixture, using a bench scraper or a pair of large metal spoons, until it is in pea-sized chunks.

2. Using a fork, stir in the egg. If the dough is too dry, add cold water, a tablespoon at a time. You should now have a dough that will just hold together. Form the dough into a disk, cover tightly in plastic wrap, and refrigerate for at least 1 hour.

3. On a clean work surface dusted with flour, roll the chilled dough into a 12-inch circle, about ⅛ inch thick. Butter a 9-inch pie pan, line it with the dough, and trim the overhang to about an inch. Tuck the overhang under itself to make a thick edge, then press it into the pan—or press the tines of a fork around the edge to decorate it. Place in the fridge or freezer to chill for another 30 minutes.

4. Heat the oven to 400°F. Line the chilled crust with foil and fill with pie weights, dried beans, or dried rice to help the crust hold its shape while baking. Bake for 15 minutes, then remove the weights and foil and bake for 10 more minutes, until the crust begins to brown lightly. Remove from the oven.

5. While the crust cools, reduce the oven heat to 350°F and make the filling. In a mixing bowl, stir together the brown sugar and melted butter. Add the maple syrup, 3 beaten eggs, toasted pecans, vanilla, pinch of salt, and ginger; stir with a large wooden spoon until the ingredients are well combined.

6. Pour the mixture into the cooled pie crust. Mix the egg and water for the egg wash and brush onto the crust edges. Bake the pie for 30 to 40 minutes, or until set. Remove from the oven and let cool on a wire rack before serving.

HORSEFEATHER

The Midwest's take on a Moscow mule, the Horsefeather is a sweet, fizzy refresher. There's debate over whether the cocktail was born in Lawrence, Kansas, or Kansas City, Missouri, but whatever its provenance, this gingery whiskey concoction is one you'll want to sip while completing your Destination Tickets.

Makes: 2 drinks
Total time: 5 minutes

4 ounces (½ cup) bourbon or whiskey

8 ounces (1 cup) ginger beer

8 dashes Angostura bitters

lime (or lemon), cut into wedges

1. Fill two highball or tall glasses with ice. In a small pitcher or large glass, combine the whiskey, ginger beer, and bitters. Squeeze in a lime wedge and gently stir.

2. Pour into the glasses and garnish with the remaining lime wedges.

Did You Know?

Ticket to Ride also exists in a more compact and quicker format. New York, London, San Francisco, or Paris versions are 10 to 15-minute games that are played on a board not larger than two US letter-sized pieces of paper.

WHITEFISH SALAD WITH CRUDITÉS

Using freshwater Great Lakes whitefish, this creamy salad is a staple of Ashkenazi Jewish American cuisine. Whether you slather it on a bagel, use it to jazz up sliced veggies, or eat it on its own, it's a must-eat when zipping through the Great Lakes region. Bonus: It's quick and easy if your game night prep is running behind schedule.

Makes: 8 servings
Active time: 20 minutes
Total time: 20 minutes

2 pounds smoked whitefish (see note)

7 celery ribs, divided

¼ cup finely chopped fresh dill

⅓ cup mayonnaise

zest of 1 lemon

2 tablespoons freshly squeezed lemon juice

4 carrots

2 cups baby bell peppers

2 cups sugar snap peas

1. Remove the skin from the whitefish. Using your fingers or a fork, pull the flesh from the bones and place in a medium bowl. Use a fork to break it into smaller pieces, removing any small bones you find.

2. Finely mince 2 celery ribs and add to the bowl along with the dill, mayonnaise, and lemon zest and juice. Gently fold everything in, taking care not to further break up the fish.

3. Peel and slice the carrots, slice the remaining 5 celery ribs and the baby bells, and serve along with the snap peas to accompany the salad.

Note
If you cannot find smoked whitefish, smoked trout makes a good substitute.

CHICAGO-STYLE DEEP DISH PIZZA

What's the best style of pizza is an enduring debate, but when riding through the Windy City there's only one right answer: deep dish. With a cornmeal-infused dough, a pound each of mozzarella and provolone blanketing the bottom, and a huge disk of Italian sausage, this is most definitely a winning combination.

Makes: 2 pizzas
Active time: 1 hour
Total time: 3 hours

CRUST

¼ ounce (2¼ teaspoons) active dry yeast

1¼ cups warm water (approximately 110°F)

1 teaspoon dark brown sugar

3¼ cups bread flour, plus more for dusting

½ cup medium-grind yellow cornmeal

2 teaspoons kosher salt

½ cup olive oil, plus more for coating the bowl

TOMATO SAUCE

2 tablespoons olive oil

1 cup diced medium, sweet onion, such as yellow or whites

4 cloves garlic, minced

1 teaspoon dried oregano

½ teaspoon crushed red pepper flakes

1 tablespoon dark brown sugar

2 teaspoons salt

¼ teaspoon smoked paprika

1. To make the dough, in the bowl of a stand mixer combine the yeast, warm water, and brown sugar. Mix and let sit for 10 minutes, until foamy.

2. Add the flour, cornmeal, 2 teaspoons salt, and ½ cup olive oil. Using a dough hook, mix on medium speed for about 8 minutes. The dough should bounce back when pressed and not stick to the sides of the bowl. (Alternatively, you can knead by hand on a floured surface until the dough comes together.)

3. Remove the dough, rub the inside of the bowl with a small amount of olive oil, and place the dough back in the bowl, turning to coat it with the oil. Cover with a towel and let rise in a warm place for at least 45 minutes, or until the dough doubles in size.

4. While the dough is rising, heat 2 tablespoons olive oil in a small saucepan over medium heat. Add the diced onion and cook until tender, stirring occasionally, about 6 minutes. Add the garlic, oregano, crushed red pepper, 1 tablespoon brown sugar, 2 teaspoons salt, and smoked paprika and cook for another minute. Add the tomatoes and basil and bring to a simmer. Cook for 30 to 40 minutes, until the sauce is slightly reduced and thickened.

5. Preheat the oven to 500°F for at least 30 minutes. Once the dough is ready, divide it in half and roll into balls, tucking the dough edges into the bottom. Let rest for 5 minutes.

1 (28-ounce) can whole peeled San Marzano tomatoes, crushed in your hands or with a potato masher

1 tablespoon chopped fresh basil

PIZZA FILLING

2 tablespoons unsalted butter, softened

¼ cup extra-virgin olive oil, plus more for bowl

1 pound sliced mozzarella cheese

1 pound sliced provolone cheese

2 pounds raw sweet Italian sausage, ground

½ cup freshly grated parmesan cheese

SPECIAL EQUIPMENT

stand mixer with a dough hook

6. Coat the bottoms and sides of two 9-inch cast-iron skillets with the 2 tablespoons butter and pour in the ¼ cup olive oil. Press the dough balls into the bottom of the pans and cover with a towel. Let sit for 15 to 20 minutes, then press the dough about 1 or 2 inches up the pan sides.

7. Layer the mozzarella and provolone cheeses on the crust, about ¼ inch higher than the dough. Press the ground sausage into large disks and place on top of the cheese. Add about 1¼ cups tomato sauce to each pizza, enough to evenly cover the meat and cheese. Sprinkle the parmesan cheese on top.

8. Bake for 25 to 35 minutes, or until the crust edges are golden brown and the filling is set. Remove from the oven and let cool for at least 10 minutes. Remove from skillets and serve hot with knife and fork.

Did You Know?

The score track that wraps around the board from 0 to 100 and the white-bordered cards have become synonymous with Ticket to Ride, but this wasn't always the case. The very first version of the game had a score track that only went up to 80 points, and the cards had a black border.

Italian Chopped Salad

When building transcontinental train tracks, you need sustenance that goes beyond a ho-hum garden salad. This Italian Chopped Salad is a satisfying mix of meat (a spicy dry salami), cheese (a creamy, fresh mozzarella is best), and an intense vinaigrette using Chicago-style giardiniera (an Italian pickled relish that Chicagoans use with just about everything).

Makes: 4 servings
Active time: 20 minutes
Total time: 20 minutes

4 romaine hearts, halved and chopped in small pieces

2 Roma tomatoes, finely diced

1 green bell pepper, finely diced

½ red onion, finely diced

⅓ cup pitted Kalamata olives, halved

8 ounces whole-milk mozzarella cheese, diced

4 ounces Italian dry salami, finely diced

1 tablespoon finely chopped fresh basil

1 tablespoon finely chopped fresh Italian parsley

kosher salt

freshly ground black pepper

1. In a large salad bowl, combine the chopped vegetables, olives, mozzarella, salami, and herbs. Pour on the vinaigrette and season with salt and pepper to taste. Serve immediately.

Italian Vinaigrette

Makes: about ½ cup

½ cup giardiniera, chopped fine

2 cloves garlic, minced

¼ teaspoon Dijon mustard

½ teaspoon salt

½ teaspoon dried oregano

½ teaspoon dried basil

½ teaspoon freshly ground pepper

1 teaspoon sugar

¼ cup red wine vinegar

¼ cup extra-virgin olive oil

1. To make the salad dressing, in a small bowl combine the chopped giardiniera, garlic, Dijon mustard, salt, oregano, basil, pepper, sugar, vinegar, and oil. Whisk to combine. The dressing will be chunky.

THIMBLEBERRY OR RASPBERRY BROWNIES

If you're lucky enough to have access to thimbleberries—the subtle, tart-sweet Midwestern berries similar to raspberries—try them swirled into a pan of rich, fudgy brownies. This recipe uses berries in three forms—fresh, freeze-dried, and jam—to really highlight the fruit flavor.

Makes: 8 servings
Active time: 15 minutes
Total time: 1 hour

1 tablespoon plus 1 cup softened unsalted butter, divided

4 eggs

2 cups sugar

1 cup self-rising flour

¾ cup cocoa powder

1 cup dark chocolate chunks

1 cup fresh thimbleberries or raspberries (see note)

½ cup freeze-dried raspberries, crushed

¼ cup raspberry jam

1. Preheat the oven to 350°F. Grease a 12 x 9-inch baking dish with 1 tablespoon butter.

2. In a large bowl, beat the 1 cup butter, eggs, sugar, flour, and cocoa powder with an electric mixer or by hand until smooth. Gently fold in the chocolate chunks and fresh berries.

3. Pour the batter into the greased pan and top with the crushed freeze-dried raspberries and dollops of jam.

4. Bake until a toothpick inserted in the center comes out clean, about 40 to 45 minutes. Let cool completely before cutting.

Note
Thimbleberries are very delicate so they're rarely produced commercially. Feel free to use raspberries for an almost-as-good result.

OLD FASHIONED

Just how popular a drink is the Old Fashioned? Depending on your source, it is either the most popular or the second most popular cocktail in the world! Yes, the US-born mixture of whiskey, sugar, bitters, and orange twist has conquered the world. This recipe is fairly, well, old fashioned—but you can shake things up by switching up the spirits and adding different flavors.

Makes: 2 drinks
Total time: 5 minutes

4 teaspoons simple syrup

4 dashes Angostura bitters

4 ounces (½ cup) rye whiskey or bourbon

orange twist

1. Pour the simple syrup and bitters into two rocks glasses. Fill the glasses halfway with ice and stir.

2. Add the whiskey or bourbon and stir again. If you're feeling adventurous, you can "flame" the orange twist. Hold a lit match several inches above the cocktail and hold the orange twist an inch above the match. Squeeze the peel to extract the oils, and then drop it into the glass.

Did You Know?

In 2014, Ticket to Ride celebrated its tenth birthday. At this occasion, a deluxe collector edition was released to pay tribute to all the families and friends who shared exciting railway adventures with each other throughout the years. It contained detailed train cars stored in elegant metal boxes, as well as an enlarged game board and brand-new illustrations. Fans of the series were delighted by this limited edition, which was only available temporarily.

WEST

DESTINATION
TICKET

VANCOUVER ◆ SANTA FE

CALIFORNIA ROLL

The California roll has been the gateway sushi for many Westerners. Reports vary, but this famous sushi roll was created sometime in the 1960s or 1970s specifically to appeal to those unfamiliar with eating raw fish. Rolling it rice-side-out hid the nori (the seaweed wrapper), and the avocado and cooked crabstick inside were familiar flavors to Western palates. Even though sushi's popularity has skyrocketed over the past decades, the California roll remains a favorite for locals and travelers alike.

Makes: 3 rolls
Active time: 15 minutes
Total time: 25 minutes

2 cups raw sushi rice

3½ tablespoons seasoned rice vinegar

3 sheets nori

sesame seeds, for sprinkling

3 to 4 crabsticks

½ cucumber, seeded and cut into matchstick-size pieces

½ avocado, thinly sliced

wasabi, for serving

pickled ginger, for serving

SPECIAL EQUIPMENT
sushi rolling mat

1. Cook the rice according to the package directions. Let cool and then stir in the rice vinegar.

2. Lay a sheet of nori shiny side down on a sushi rolling mat. Spread a handful of the cooked rice over the nori, lightly pressing it down. Sprinkle with sesame seeds. Then turn the nori over so the shiny side faces up and the rice faces down.

3. About 1 to 2 inches above the bottom edge of the nori sheet, arrange a crabstick horizontally across the sheet. Above that place a row of cucumber pieces, then a row of avocado slices.

4. Holding onto the mat edge closest to you, roll the filled nori into a tight cylinder.

5. Repeat for the remaining 2 rolls, then slice each roll into 6 to 8 pieces. Serve with a dollop of wasabi and pickled ginger on the side.

Baja Fish Tacos

Bring the beach to wherever you're gaming with these Baja Fish Tacos. Crunchy and tasty, they pack a major flavor punch with a super-creamy sauce and just the right amount of heat. This recipe uses halibut, which swim all along the California coast and down through Baja, but really, you can use any mild white fish.

Makes: 6 tacos
Active time: 30 minutes
Total time: 1 hour 30 minutes

¼ red cabbage, thinly sliced (about 1½ cups)

4 limes, divided

kosher salt, to taste

½ cup Mexican crema or sour cream

1 egg

1 cup lager beer

½ teaspoon chipotle chili powder

freshly ground pepper, to taste

1 tablespoon honey or agave nectar

1 cup flour

vegetable oil, for frying

1¼ pounds skinless halibut fillet, cut into 2-inch strips

6 flour tortillas

1 avocado

½ cup salsa verde (for a recipe, see Christmas Salsas and Chips, page 131)

1 cup roughly chopped fresh cilantro

1. In a small bowl, mix the sliced cabbage with the zest and juice of 1 lime and a sprinkle of kosher salt until the cabbage is covered with the liquid. Cover and put in the refrigerator for at least an hour but up to 4. Drain the pickled cabbage before serving.

2. In another small bowl, mix the crema with the zest and juice of 1 lime. Slice the remaining two limes into wedges.

3. Mix the batter by whisking the egg, beer, chipotle chili powder, salt, pepper, and agave in a large shallow bowl. Once combined, add the flour and whisk until smooth.

4. In a medium pot, heat approximately 4 inches of vegetable oil over medium heat until a deep-fry thermometer registers 375°F. Dip the fish in the batter, then fry in batches in the hot oil until golden and just cooked through, 3 to 5 minutes per batch. Transfer with a slotted spoon to a paper-towel-lined plate to drain. Season with more salt.

5. Toast each tortilla quickly in a skillet over medium-high heat until slightly charred but still flexible.

6. Halve, pit, and slice the avocado. Fill the tortillas with the fish, avocado slices, pickled cabbage, and salsa verde. Drizzle with Mexican crema, top with cilantro, and serve with lime wedges.

Guacamole and Chips

Warning: This guac is so good that you might be asked to host all future game nights. Crunchy pepitas and ruby red grapefruit brighten the dip, while the chipotle and garlic-spiced chips make for an excellent scooping vessel. (Feel free to cheat and buy your chips; just don't cheat in the game!)

Makes: 6 servings
Total time: 45 minutes

½ cup raw pepitas (pumpkin seeds)

2 tablespoons kosher salt, plus more for seasoning

1 tablespoon garlic powder (black garlic powder optional)

1 tablespoon chipotle powder

1 lime

1 ruby red grapefruit

2 serrano or jalapeño chiles

1 small white onion

6 cloves garlic

4 avocados

5 stalks cilantro (leaves only)

4 cups peanut oil

6 flour tortillas

1. Toast the pepitas in a small dry pan over medium-high heat and then set aside to cool.

2. To make the spice mix, add 2 tablespoons salt, the garlic powder (or black garlic powder, for even more flavor), and the chipotle powder to a small bowl. Zest the lime into the bowl and mix to combine, then set aside.

3. Next juice the lime into a separate small bowl. Supreme the grapefruit by removing the skin and white pith and cutting out the individual segments between the membranes. Then chop into ¼-inch pieces and set aside.

4. Halve and deseed the chiles and remove the skin from the onion. Roughly chop the chiles and onion and add to a food processor or blender along with the peeled garlic cloves. Pulse until minced but not yet a paste—5 to 10 pulses, depending on your machine.

5. Halve and pit the avocados, then scoop out the flesh, place in a large bowl, and mash with a potato masher to your desired level of chunkiness. Add in the reserved lime juice, minced onion mix, and pepitas. Mix to combine and season to taste with salt. Add the grapefruit pieces and cilantro leaves and transfer to a serving bowl. (Note: If you are doing this ahead of time, add extra lime juice or press plastic wrap directly onto the guacamole to prevent oxidation.)

6. To make the chips, in a large pot heat the peanut oil over medium-high heat to 350°F. Slice the flour tortillas in half and then crosswise into 1-inch-wide strips. Working in batches, fry the strips for 1 to 2 minutes, until golden brown.

7. Remove from the oil to a paper-towel-lined baking sheet. Sprinkle with the spice mix. Serve the chips warm alongside the guacamole.

MISSION FIG AND ALMOND CAKE

Didn't complete all your routes? Everyone wins with this fig and almond upside-down cake. California grows a whopping 98 percent of all the fresh figs in the US, so if that's your destination, you'll definitely want to stuff some into your suitcase.

Makes: 1 (9-inch) cake
Active time: 20 minutes
Total time: 1 hour 15 minutes

8 tablespoons (1 stick) unsalted butter, divided

½ cup light or dark brown sugar, packed

12 fresh figs

1 cup raw almonds

¼ cup granulated sugar

¼ cup flour

½ teaspoon baking powder

⅛ teaspoon salt

2 eggs, at room temperature

½ cup sour cream, at room temperature

2 tablespoons honey

1 teaspoon vanilla extract

½ teaspoon almond extract

1. Preheat the oven to 350°F. Line the bottom of a 9-inch cake pan with parchment paper, then grease the parchment and pan edges.

2. In a small saucepan over low heat, melt 4 tablespoons of the butter. Stir in the brown sugar and then pour the mixture into the prepared cake pan.

3. Remove the stems and slice the figs in half lengthwise. Arrange them cut-side down in the cake pan in concentric circles.

4. In a food processor or blender, grind the almonds and sugar together into a powder. Add the flour, baking powder, and salt and pulse to combine.

5. Melt the remaining 4 tablespoons butter in a small pan over low heat. In a large bowl, whisk the melted butter with the eggs, sour cream, honey, vanilla, and almond extract. Add the almond mixture from the food processor and beat with a whisk until just incorporated.

6. Gently pour the batter evenly over the figs in the cake pan. Bake for 30 to 35 minutes, until a toothpick comes out clean and the edges start to pull away from the pan. Cool on a wire rack for at least 20 minutes before inverting the cake onto a serving dish.

MAI TAI

It was 1944 in Oakland, California, when Victor "Trader Vic" Bergeron put the Mai Tai on the map. And if your map takes you along the Pacific coast, you'll want to have one of these boozy cocktails in hand. This version keeps it fresh with just a little lime juice and a whole lot of rum. Garnish with bright cherries, mint, and a pineapple wedge to make it extra beachy.

Makes: 2 drinks
Total time: 5 minutes

3 ounces (6 tablespoons) white rum

1½ ounces (3 tablespoons) orange curaçao

1½ ounces (3 tablespoons) freshly squeezed lime juice

1 ounce (2 tablespoons) orgeat syrup

1½ ounces (3 tablespoons) dark rum

pineapple wedges, for garnish

maraschino cherries, for garnish

mint, for garnish

1. In a shaker filled with crushed ice, pour the white rum, curaçao, lime juice, and orgeat. Lightly shake.

2. Pour the drinks with the ice into rocks glasses and then slowly pour ¾ ounce of dark rum over each drink. Garnish with a pineapple wedge, cherry, and mint.

SMOKED SALMON CUCUMBER BITES

Salmon is an essential—and delicious—part of Pacific Northwest cuisine. In fact, many riders plan their routes through this region just for the fish. To preserve it beyond the summer season, smoked salmon has become a way of life. In this easy appetizer, the velvety fish melds perfectly with the richness of the cream cheese, and the pop of the cool cucumber freshens it up.

Makes: about 20 bites
Active time: 15 minutes
Total time: 15 minutes

4 ounces cream cheese, softened or whipped

½ teaspoon lemon juice

½ teaspoon Dijon mustard

2 green onions, greens finely chopped

1 tablespoon chopped fresh dill, plus extra sprigs for garnish

salt and pepper, to taste

1 English cucumber, cut in ½-inch-thick slices

4 ounces smoked salmon, cut into bite-sized pieces

1. Combine the cream cheese, lemon juice, mustard, green onions, dill, salt, and pepper in a small bowl and mix with a large spoon until smooth.

2. Place a dollop of the cream cheese mixture onto each cucumber slice. Next top with a slice of the smoked salmon and garnish with a sprig of dill.

Did You Know?
Game creator and author Alan R. Moon has said, "I love route-building games and I love railroads so my goal with Ticket to Ride was to design a game that combined those two things in the simplest way possible, while retaining a game that was fun to play no matter how many times you played it."

CRAB PASTA

Adding crab to your pasta when you're riding along the West Coast just makes sense. The briny, meaty crustacean combined with a warm, inviting bowl of noodles is the perfect pick-me-up after someone blocks your route. This take is updated with a spicy sauce inspired by Singapore chili crab, which originated in Singapore in the 1950s and has made its way to the coastal cities of California.

Makes: 4 servings
Active time: 30 minutes
Total time: 30 minutes

4 quarts water

2 tablespoons salt

1 pound pappardelle (or another wide, long noodle, such as fettuccine)

7 tablespoons peanut oil

2 to 3 shallots, minced (about ½ cup)

1½-inch ginger knob, peeled and grated (about 2 tablespoons)

6 medium cloves garlic, minced (about 2 tablespoons)

2 Thai (bird's eye) chiles, minced (optional)

¼ cup tomato paste

1 cup chicken broth

1 pound cooked or canned lump crab meat

½ cup sambal chili sauce, or more as desired

1 tablespoon sugar

½ cup thinly sliced green onions, stems and greens combined

1 cup fresh cilantro leaves

1. Bring the water to a boil in a large pot, adding the 2 tablespoons salt. Add the pasta and cook according to the package directions until not quite al dente—about 2 minutes before the directions say it will be ready. Drain, reserving 1 cup of the pasta water.

2. In a large wok or Dutch oven, heat the peanut oil over medium heat until shimmering. Stir in the shallots, grated ginger, garlic, and chiles (if you want it extra spicy). Cook, stirring, until fragrant, about 1 minute.

3. Stir in the tomato paste and cook for 1 more minute. Add the broth and increase the heat to medium high. Bring to a boil and cook until the mixture is reduced by half, about 6 minutes.

4. Reduce the heat to low and gently fold in the crab pieces, trying not to break them up much. Stir in the chili sauce and sugar. Simmer 1 minute and season to taste with salt and/or extra chili.

5. Add the cooked pasta to the sauce, along with some of the reserved cooking water (½ cup or more). Simmer for 1 more minute, until the sauce comes together and the pasta is fully al dente. Ladle into a serving dish and sprinkle with the green onions and cilantro.

WILD BERRY SALAD

If your travels take you to Oregon between June and August, you'll see berries as bright as your train cars bursting from bushes and vines. The marionberries (a firm, sweet-tart type of blackberry), raspberries, and strawberries that flourish in the Pacific Northwest are among the sweetest, juiciest bites of summer you'll ever eat. And while they're amazing on their own, they really brighten up this spinach salad, dressed with a blackberry balsamic vinaigrette.

Makes: 4 servings
Active time: 15 minutes
Total time: 15 minutes

4 cups baby spinach

1½ cups berries, such as raspberries, strawberries, marionberries, or other blackberries

⅓ cup crumbled blue cheese

⅓ cup chopped hazelnuts, lightly toasted

BLACKBERRY BALSAMIC VINAIGRETTE

¾ cup blackberries

2 teaspoons sugar

2 tablespoons balsamic vinegar

2 tablespoons olive oil

¼ teaspoon salt

¼ teaspoon pepper

1. Toss the spinach, 1½ cups of berries, blue cheese, and hazelnuts together in a large bowl.

2. To make the vinaigrette, place the ¾ cup blackberries, sugar, balsamic vinegar, olive oil, salt, and pepper in the bowl of a food processor. Mix until well combined, then drizzle onto the salad to serve.

HAZELNUT COFFEE CAKE

A staggering 99 percent of US hazelnuts—also known as filberts— are grown in Oregon's Willamette Valley. So yes, it's safe to say that the Pacific Northwest is big on these sweet, earthy nuts. They add just the right amount of crunch to the brown sugar and cinnamon filling and topping for this glazed sour cream coffee cake, a perfect nibbler throughout your game.

Makes: 1 (9½-inch) cake
Active time: 20 minutes
Total time: 1 hour 5 minutes

½ cup (1 stick) unsalted butter, at room temperature

1 cup granulated sugar

2 eggs

1 teaspoon vanilla extract

1 cup (½ pint) sour cream

1 teaspoon baking powder

1 teaspoon baking soda

½ teaspoon salt

2 cups flour

⅔ cup light or dark brown sugar

2 teaspoons ground cinnamon

½ cup rough-chopped hazelnuts, skins removed and lightly toasted

GLAZE
¾ cup powdered sugar

1 tablespoon unsalted butter, melted

¼ cup whole milk

1 teaspoon vanilla extract

SPECIAL EQUIPMENT
9½-inch tube pan

1. In a large bowl, cream the butter and sugar with an electric mixer until well combined. Mix in the eggs until thoroughly combined. Add the vanilla and sour cream and mix until well incorporated.

2. Add the baking powder, baking soda, salt, and flour and mix until just combined. The batter should be thick.

3. Preheat the oven to 350°F. In a small bowl, mix together the brown sugar, cinnamon, and chopped hazelnuts—this will be your filling and topping.

4. Grease a 9½-inch tube pan and spread half the batter in the pan. Sprinkle half the hazelnut filling over it, then spread the rest of the batter on top. Sprinkle the remaining hazelnut mixture on top.

5. Bake for 45 minutes, then transfer the cake to a cooling rack. To make the glaze, mix the powdered sugar, butter, milk, and vanilla into a thick syrup with a large spoon. Once the cake is cool, remove from pan and drizzle the glaze over the top.

Espresso Martini

Seattle has been coffee-crazed since 1895, when someone picked up some spilled beans and decided to pan-roast them. (And then, of course, there's a certain coffee behemoth that has long made the city its home.) But to add even more buzz to your buzz, nothing beats an espresso martini. This strong yet smooth sip is guaranteed to get you energized enough to snatch up the Longest Continuous Path bonus card.

Makes: 2 drinks
Total time: 5 minutes

4 ounces (½ cup) vodka

1 ounce (2 tablespoons) coffee liqueur

2 ounces (4 tablespoons) freshly brewed espresso

1 ounce (2 tablespoons) simple syrup

espresso beans, for garnish

1. Fill a shaker with a few ice cubes and then pour in the vodka, coffee liqueur, espresso, and simple syrup. Shake until well chilled and foamy, about 20 seconds.

2. Strain into two chilled martini glasses and garnish with espresso beans.

Did You Know?
The man who's been at the drafting table for almost the entire Ticket to Ride series is Julien Delval (the only exception is the First Journey series). The style of his graphics, his technique (in gouache), and his brightly colored characters have become trademarks of the series.

WEST

WILD MUSHROOM CROSTINI

In the dark, wet conifer forests of the Rocky Mountains, wild things grow. Cordyceps, chanterelles, morels, oysters, and porcinis—these little fungi pop up on logs and in clearings, and they're delicious when cooked with butter, white wine, and cream. Crowning slices of toasty baguette, this rich appetizer will fuel any adventure. If you're out in the wild gathering mushrooms, make sure your travel companion is an experienced hunter, otherwise "wild" mushrooms can be found in your local grocery store.

Makes: 4 servings
Active time: 10 minutes
Total time: 10 to 15 minutes

3 tablespoons unsalted butter

1 shallot, chopped

2 cups mixed "wild" mushrooms, such as porcini, oyster, and chanterelle

2 cloves garlic, minced

3 tablespoons dry white wine

2 tablespoons heavy cream

1 baguette, cut into ½-inch slices

2 tablespoons olive oil

⅓ cup shredded parmesan cheese

1. Heat the butter in a medium skillet over medium-high heat. Add the chopped shallot and cook for 1 minute.

2. Add the mushrooms whole and cook for 4 to 6 minutes, stirring occasionally. Next stir in the garlic and wine and cook for 1 minute more. Remove from the heat and stir in the cream.

3. Set the oven to broil. Brush the bread slices with the olive oil. Then place the slices on a baking sheet and top with the mushroom mixture. Sprinkle the parmesan on top and broil for about 2 minutes, until the cheese is melted.

SKILLET TROUT

If you're looking for the perfect protein, this fish could be just the ticket. Many species of trout are native to the cold rivers snaking through the Rockies—and if you look out of your window as you chug along the Colorado River, you might even see some jumping. The simple, clean flavors in this dish highlight the mild, flaky rainbow trout, and the fennel gives it some bite.

Makes: 4 servings
Active time: 15 to 20 minutes
Total time: 15 to 20 minutes

4 rainbow trout fillets

salt and pepper, to taste

4 tablespoons olive oil, divided

2 lemons, 1 juiced and 1 sliced

3 cloves garlic, minced

1 teaspoon chopped fresh dill

1 whole fennel bulb

1 teaspoon chopped fennel fronds

2 tablespoons unsalted butter

1. Pat the trout pieces dry and season both sides with salt and pepper.

2. In a small bowl, mix 2 tablespoons olive oil and the juice of 1 lemon with the garlic, dill, and 1 teaspoon chopped fennel fronds. Brush onto the fish.

3. Prepare the fennel bulb by cutting it in half, removing the core, and slicing it into half-inch segments. Toss the slices with the remaining 2 tablespoons olive oil and add salt and pepper to taste.

4. Preheat a medium skillet over medium-high heat. Add the fennel segments and lemon slices. Char the lemon for about 1 minute and remove; roast the fennel for at least 5 minutes per side, until nicely charred. Remove from the skillet.

5. Melt the butter in the skillet and then add the trout, skin side down. Cook for 3 to 4 minutes, then flip and cook for 2½ minutes, skin side up. Top with the lemon slices and serve with fennel.

ROASTED ROOT VEGETABLES

Root crops such as carrots, turnips, beets, onions, potatoes, and parsnips thrive at high altitudes. Besides being plentiful, they're also pretty darn tasty, especially when roasted with olive oil, fresh rosemary, and thyme. Not to mention, they'll give you a hearty boost of energy the next time someone blocks your path and you have to find an alternative route.

Makes: 6 to 8 servings
Active time: 10 minutes
Total time: 50 minutes

2 pounds root vegetables, such as carrots, parsnips, beets, and potatoes

1 red onion

¼ cup olive oil

salt and pepper, to taste

1 teaspoon minced fresh rosemary

1 teaspoon minced fresh thyme

1. Preheat the oven to 425°F. Peel and cut the root vegetables, including the onion, into 1 to 2-inch chunks.

2. Place the cut vegetables on a rimmed baking sheet and drizzle with the olive oil. Sprinkle with salt and pepper. Bake for 30 minutes, until beginning to get tender.

3. Sprinkle with the rosemary and thyme and cook for another 10 minutes, then transfer to a bowl to serve.

Did You Know?
Each game box shows a steam train surrounded by characters who are (almost always) holding a train ticket. This visual cohesion ensures people can recognize a box from the Ticket to Ride series in the blink of an eye.

WILD BERRY CAKE

Berries such as raspberries and blackberries grow well at high altitudes and can actually taste sweeter than their lowland counterparts. While they're delicious plucked straight from the bush or vine, they're even better swirled into this vanilla cake—an easy-eating treat for all the route builders around your table.

Makes: 1 (9-inch) cake
Active time: 15 minutes
Total time: 45 to 50 minutes

2 cups flour

1 cup sugar

2 teaspoons baking powder

1 teaspoon salt

2 eggs, at room temperature

1 teaspoon vanilla extract

½ cup (1 stick) unsalted butter, melted

½ cup whole milk, at room temperature

½ cup sour cream, at room temperature

1 teaspoon lemon zest

2 cups mixed berries, tossed in 2 teaspoons flour

powdered sugar, for dusting

1. Preheat the oven to 350°F. Grease a 9-inch cake pan.

2. In a large bowl, mix together the flour, sugar, baking powder, and salt. Add the eggs, vanilla, butter, milk, sour cream, and lemon zest and stir with a large spoon until just combined.

3. Gently fold in the floured berries (tossing them in flour reduces the moisture and keeps the cake from collapsing). Pour the batter into the prepared cake pan.

4. Bake for 30 to 35 minutes, until the sides start to pull away from the pan and a toothpick inserted in the middle comes out clean. Place on a rack and let cool. Remove from the pan then sprinkle with powdered sugar.

ROOT BEER FLOAT

Brewery owner Frank J. Wisner was looking to create a drink inspired by his surrounding snow-covered Rocky Mountains. Foamy root beer with ice cream "peaks" fit the bill, and in 1893 the root beer float was born in Cripple Creek, Colorado. Who wouldn't want this sweet drink/dessert waiting for them when they pull into the station?

Makes: 2 floats
Total time: 5 minutes

4 to 6 scoops vanilla ice cream

16 ounces (2 cups) root beer

3 ounces (6 tablespoons) vanilla vodka or spirit of choice (optional)

maraschino cherries, for garnish

1. About 20 minutes before you want to drink your floats, place two tall glasses in the freezer to get nice and frosty.

2. Fill each chilled glass with 2 to 3 scoops of vanilla ice cream. Slowly pour a cup of root beer into each mug. (If adding vodka, pour in a shot halfway through.) Top each drink with a cherry.

Did You Know?
Ticket to Ride has a legacy edition. Ticket to Ride® Legacy: Legends of the West follows a story over a series of 12 games. As you progress through the story, new game elements are unlocked, rules change, and the game board is permanently altered.

Classic Cobb Salad

Straight from Hollywood's famous original Brown Derby restaurant, the Cobb is the original chopped salad. Loaded with chicken, eggs, bacon, blue cheese, and a dressing that uses both lemon and vinegar to temper all that richness, this celebrity-status salad should be the first thing you order in the dining car if you're traveling in style.

Makes: 4 servings
Active time: 30 minutes
Total time: 2 hours

½ cup apple cider vinegar

½ cup extra-virgin olive oil

1 clove garlic, chopped

2 teaspoons salt, divided

2 teaspoons pepper, divided

1 teaspoon dried thyme

zest and juice of 1 lemon, divided

½ teaspoon garlic powder

1 teaspoon harissa spice blend

4 boneless, skinless chicken breasts

4 eggs

12 slices bacon

2 avocados

2 heads romaine lettuce

2 cups cherry tomatoes, cut in half

8 ounces blue cheese

OPTIONAL SPECIAL EQUIPMENT
sous vide immersion circulator

1. To make the dressing, in a small bowl combine the vinegar, olive oil, garlic, 1 teaspoon salt, 1 teaspoon pepper, thyme, and lemon zest and juice (reserving a teaspoon of juice). Whisk vigorously to blend, then set aside to let the flavors meld.

2. In a separate small bowl, make a spice mix for the chicken by combining the remaining salt and pepper with the garlic powder and harissa. Pat the chicken breasts dry with a paper towel and season on all sides with the spice mix.

3. Place the chicken in a ziplock plastic bag and use a sous vide machine to cook it in a water bath for 1½ hours at 145°F. After 30 minutes, add the whole eggs directly to the water and cook with the chicken for the remaining 1 hour. Once complete, remove from the water bath and set aside to cool. (Alternatively, you can poach the chicken and eggs in simmering water for approximately 10 minutes until the internal temperature of the chicken reaches 170°F.)

4. Fry the bacon in a large skillet on medium-high heat until crispy and then remove it to a paper-towel-lined plate.

5. Cut the avocados in half, remove the pits, and slice (in the skin) into thin strips. Using a spoon, remove the flesh. Sprinkle the cut avocado slices with the reserved teaspoon of lemon juice to prevent browning.

6. To make the salad, chop the romaine lettuce into small strips and place in a large bowl. Mix in half of the dressing.

7. Cut the cooked chicken breasts into strips and cut the eggs in half lengthwise; arrange on top of the lettuce. Add to the salad along with the tomatoes, crispy bacon slices, avocado slices, and blue cheese crumbles. Top with the rest of the dressing to serve.

CHATEAUBRIAND

Nothing says "first class" quite like filet mignon. Inspired by the glitz and glam of a stop in Las Vegas, this reverse-seared steak is gilded with edible gold leaf and served with a rich, creamy sauce. Don't be intimidated by its fancy looks—this is an easy preparation, and you can order edible gold leaf inexpensively online.

Makes: 4 servings
Active time: 15 minutes
Total time: 1 hour

4 filet mignon steaks, approximately 4 ounces each

2 tablespoons plus 1 teaspoon kosher salt, divided

2 tablespoons plus 1 teaspoon coarsely ground black pepper, divided

4 tablespoons (½ stick) unsalted butter, divided

2 tablespoons olive oil

¾ cup chopped shallots (3 to 4 shallots)

3 cloves garlic

1 cup beef broth

½ cup cognac or sherry

8 sheets edible gold leaf (optional)

1. Preheat the oven to 200°F. For a perfectly cooked medium-rare steak, use a reverse sear method—cooking the meat slowly in a low-heat oven and finishing over high heat.

2. Thoroughly dry the steaks with paper towels and sprinkle the surfaces with 2 tablespoons each of salt and pepper. Put the seasoned steaks on a baking sheet and place in the oven for 45 minutes.

3. Remove the steaks from the oven and set them aside while you prepare a sauté pan. The steaks are just warmed through at this point and will finish cooking in the pan.

4. Heat 2 tablespoons butter and oil in a large sauté pan over medium-high heat until the butter is almost smoking. Place the steaks in the hot pan and sear all sides until they are a deep brown, about 1 to 2 minutes per side. Remove and let rest on a plate while you make the sauce.

5. Pour all but 2 tablespoons of the fat from the sauté pan. Add the shallots and whole garlic and cook over medium heat for 2 minutes. Add the beef broth and cook over high heat for 5 minutes until reduced by half, scraping the brown bits from the bottom of the pan. Add the cognac and cook for 2 more minutes. Remove from the heat and swirl in the remaining 2 tablespoons butter and 1 teaspoon each of salt and pepper.

6. Using a pastry brush, place one or two sheets of edible gold leaf on the surface of each steak (they should stick instantly). Serve the gilded steaks hot, on top of the sauce.

FRIES WITH UTAH FRY SAUCE

You haven't fully experienced Utah until you've dipped your french fries in the state's namesake sauce. Though the pink combination of mayonnaise and ketchup is eaten pretty much anywhere that has train tracks, Utah ups its fry-sauce game with Worcestershire sauce, smoked paprika, and onion powder to create layers of spice and tang.

Makes: 4 servings
Active time: 30 minutes
Total time: 1 hour 30 minutes

4 large russet potatoes

1 cup mayonnaise

½ cup ketchup

1 teaspoon Worcestershire sauce

2 teaspoons red wine vinegar

1 teaspoon onion powder

1 teaspoon smoked paprika

½ teaspoon garlic powder

4 quarts peanut oil (or other oil with a high smoke point)

2 teaspoons salt

1. Peel and slice the potatoes into ¼-inch-wide planks. (Using a mandolin with a slicing blade makes this easy.) Immediately place in a bowl of cold water and rinse the starch off the slices until the water runs clear. Let the potatoes sit in the cold water for at least an hour to remove excess starch, making for a crispier fry.

2. To make the sauce, in a small bowl mix together the mayonnaise, ketchup, Worcestershire sauce, red wine vinegar, onion powder, smoked paprika, and garlic powder. Set aside to let the flavors marry for at least 30 minutes.

3. Pour the oil into a large heavy-bottomed pot and heat over medium-high heat until the oil reaches 300°F.

4. Line a baking sheet with paper towels. Working in batches, fry the potato slices for 5 to 6 minutes. Then remove from the oil and increase the heat until the oil reaches 400°F. Fry the potatoes in batches a second time until golden brown, about 5 minutes per batch. Transfer the fries to the lined baking sheet and sprinkle with salt while hot. Serve with the sauce.

UTAH SCONE

If you're riding through England and order a scone, you'll get a crumbly pastry made to complement tea. But if you're riding through the western state of Utah, a scone is a little different. A literal hot take on a scone, Utah's version was likely inspired by Latter-Day Saints on missionary trips to the Southwest, where they encountered Navajo fry bread. These sweet treats are crispy and bubbly and are made even better with rich honey butter.

Makes: 8 servings
Active time: 30 minutes
Total time: 1 hour 10 minutes

1 cup warm water, divided

1 tablespoon active dry yeast

pinch plus ¼ cup plus 1 tablespoon granulated sugar, divided

⅓ cup cooking oil, for dough

1½ teaspoons salt, divided

1 egg, beaten

3½ cups flour

½ cup (1 stick) unsalted room temperature butter

1 tablespoon honey

2 quarts (8 cups) peanut oil, for frying

1. Mix 3 tablespoons of the warm water with the yeast in a small bowl, adding a pinch of sugar. Set aside for 10 minutes; the mixture will rise and foam.

2. While the yeast is rising, in a large bowl combine the remaining water with the ⅓ cup oil, 1 teaspoon salt, ¼ cup sugar, and beaten egg. Stir well and then add in the yeast mixture. Gradually add the flour, mixing well with hands after each addition.

3. On a smooth, floured surface, knead the dough until it comes together, about 5 minutes. Place in a well-greased bowl, turning so the top is greased. Cover and let rise for about 30 minutes, or until doubled in size.

4. Meanwhile, in a separate small bowl stir together the butter, remaining 1 tablespoon sugar, honey, and remaining ½ teaspoon salt. Set aside.

5. While the dough is rising, line a baking sheet with paper towels. Fill a large saucepan with 2 inches of peanut oil and heat to 350°F over medium-high heat.

6. While the oil heats, punch down the raised dough and divide it into 8 balls. On a lightly floured surface, roll the dough pieces into ¼-inch-thick circles or squares; use your fingers to stretch them out.

7. With tongs, carefully place the flattened disks in the hot oil, one at a time, and fry until golden brown on each side, about 1 to 2 minutes. Transfer to paper towels to drain. Serve hot with the honey butter.

MOSCOW MULE

Any train's bar car that's worth its copper mugs will make a killer Moscow mule. This classic cocktail uses only four ingredients, so spring for quality here. Besides zinging up your drink with flavor, the fresh ginger and lime will have your bar car smelling great.

Makes: 2 drinks
Total time: 5 minutes

zest and 1 ounce (2 tablespoons) juice from 1 lime

2 (1-inch) ginger knobs

4 ounces (½ cup) vodka

8 ounces (1 cup) ginger beer

1. Zest the lime into a small bowl. Then slice the lime in half and juice it into a separate bowl.

2. In a cocktail shaker, mix one of the ginger knobs and 2 large ice cubes. Cover and shake vigorously to release the flavor of the ginger. Add the vodka and 2 tablespoons lime juice. Vigorously shake for 1 minute.

3. Fill two copper mugs with ice. Strain half the vodka mixture into each mug and top with the ginger beer. Grate some fresh ginger on top, sprinkle with the lime zest, and serve.

WEST

CHEESE CRISPS

Ever wish nachos were just one huge, pizza-sized chip that you could devour all on your own—or, if you're feeling generous, share with your fellow competitors? Arizona does it right with cheese crisps, a sort of modified quesadilla spruced up with the addition of caramelized onions and roasted green chiles.

Makes: 1 crisp
Active time: 15 minutes
Total time: 1 hour

2 yellow onions, thinly sliced

2 red onions, thinly sliced

1 teaspoon salt

3 tablespoons unsalted butter, divided

¼ cup water

1 large flour tortilla (13-inch diameter or larger)

½ cup grated Mexican-style cheese blend or cheddar

1 (4-ounce) can roasted green chiles

1. Add the onions to a large sauté pan over medium-high heat along with the salt, 2 tablespoons butter, and water. Once the onions are translucent (but not brown) and the water is mostly evaporated, reduce the heat to medium-low and slow-cook the onions for 45 minutes, stirring every 5 to 10 minutes. Remove from heat once they've turned a dark golden brown.

2. Preheat the oven to 350°F. If using fresh chiles, slice and seed them and then roast for 10 minutes.

3. Using a pastry brush, lightly spread the remaining 1 tablespoon butter on both sides of the tortilla and place it on a cookie sheet. Bake for 6 minutes, until the edges are slightly brown, and then remove from the oven.

4. Flip the tortilla over and add the grated cheese in an even layer, then the chopped green chiles and caramelized onions. Return to the oven and cook for 5 to 7 more minutes, until the cheese is melted.

5. Remove from the oven, place on a cutting board, and cut into slices (a pizza wheel works well for this).

Chicken Enchiladas

Every region in North America has its own take on the classic comfort food casserole, and the Southwest is no exception. Theirs is just a little spicier! Green chiles add some fire to this cheesy dish, while Mexican crema or sour cream cools it down. This is the perfect make-ahead dish, so come game time your focus can be solely on cutting off your opponents' routes.

Makes: 6 to 8 servings
Active time: 30 minutes
Total time: 1 hour 15 minutes

5 tablespoons unsalted butter, divided

1 large yellow onion, minced

¼ teaspoon chipotle peppers in adobo, chopped, or chipotle powder

¼ cup flour

2 cloves garlic, chopped

½ cup chopped green chiles, freshly roasted or canned

2 cups chicken stock

1 cup half-and-half

2 teaspoons salt

1 teaspoon pepper

1 teaspoon ground cumin

12 to 15 corn tortillas

1 pound rotisserie or smoked chicken meat, shredded

3 cups shredded cheese (cheddar, monterey jack, or Mexican blend)

¼ cup Mexican crema or sour cream

¼ cup chopped cilantro

¼ cup chopped green onions

1. To a large sauté pan over medium-high heat, add 1 tablespoon of the butter and the minced yellow onion. Cook until golden brown, 5 to 7 minutes, stirring occasionally. Add the chipotles in adobo or chipotle powder and cook for an additional minute, then transfer to a bowl and set aside.

2. Using the same pan, combine the flour and remaining 4 tablespoons butter and cook until the flour is no longer raw, about 5 minutes, stirring occasionally. Add the garlic and chiles and sauté until fragrant, about a minute longer.

3. Slowly add in the chicken stock, whisking to avoid lumps. Add the half-and-half, salt, pepper, and cumin. Reduce to medium-low heat and cook for 5 more minutes, stirring occasionally, then transfer the sauce to a bowl and let cool.

4. Preheat the oven to 350°F and butter a 9 x 12-inch baking dish. To assemble the casserole, create a single layer of 3 or 4 tortillas on the bottom of the dish, cutting them as needed to fit and avoid overlapping. Spoon a quarter of the sauce over the tortilla layer, then top with a third of the shredded chicken and chipotle-onion mix, then a quarter of the cheese. Repeat the process to create three layers of tortillas, sauce, chicken, and chipotle-onion. Top with a final layer of tortillas, covered with the remaining sauce and cheese.

5. Cover with foil and bake for 30 minutes, then uncover and bake an additional 15 minutes. To serve, top with Mexican crema, chopped cilantro, and green onions.

CHRISTMAS SALSAS AND CHIPS

If your route takes you to a restaurant in New Mexico, you might be asked, "Green, red, or Christmas?" No, they're not asking about holidays. They're talking chiles, a staple of Southwestern cuisine, with "Christmas" being a colloquial term for mixing red and green chiles. The two salsas here are each delicious on their own, but even better when offered together, Christmas style.

Makes: 6 servings
Active time: 15 minutes
Total time: 1 hour

SALSA ROJA

2 guajillo chiles

1 pasilla chile

2 cloves garlic

1 tablespoon sesame seeds

1 yellow onion, roughly chopped

2 tablespoons chopped cilantro, including stems

1 cup water

1 tablespoon vegetable oil

2 teaspoons salt, or as needed

SALSA VERDE

2 serrano or jalapeño chiles, stemmed

6 cloves garlic, peeled

8 tomatillos, skins removed

1 yellow onion, roughly chopped

zest and juice of 1 lime

2 teaspoons salt

CHIPS

12 corn tortillas

zest of 1 lime

2 tablespoons salt

1 teaspoon chipotle powder

6 to 8 cups peanut oil

1. For the salsa roja, in a medium-size dry skillet over medium-high heat toast the guajillo and pasilla chiles, the 2 garlic cloves, and the sesame seeds until lightly browned and fragrant, about 2 minutes, stirring occasionally.

2. Pour the warm ingredients into a blender and add 1 chopped onion, the cilantro leaves and stems, water, oil, and 2 teaspoons salt. Blend until smooth, then taste and add more salt if needed. Transfer to a small bowl and place in the refrigerator until ready to serve.

3. For the salsa verde, cut the chiles in half lengthwise and place them on a foil-lined baking sheet along with the 6 garlic cloves, the tomatillos, and 1 chopped onion. Broil on high until slightly charred, about 5 to 7 minutes, turning once halfway through.

4. Transfer the charred vegetables to a bowl, cover with plastic wrap, and let steam for 10 minutes. Then use a mortar and pestle or food processor to roughly chop them. Return to the bowl and stir in the lime zest and juice and the 2 teaspoons salt. Let rest in the refrigerator to allow the flavors to meld until ready to serve, about 45 minutes.

5. To make the chips, cut the tortillas into quarters. In a small bowl, make the seasoning blend by combining the lime zest, 1 tablespoon salt, and the chipotle powder.

6. In a large heavy-bottomed pot, preheat 6 to 8 cups of peanut oil to 400°F. Working in batches, fry the tortillas (this goes fast—about 30 seconds per batch). Immediately after they turn a golden brown, strain them from the oil using a spider strainer and place on a metal rack over a baking sheet. Sprinkle with the seasoning blend and serve with the salsas.

SOPAPILLAS AND HONEY

Maybe the most famous of all fried breads, sopapillas finish off many meals in New Mexico. These crispy, chewy pillows of dough are even better when topped with hot honey. Just don't let it drip all over your trains!

> Makes: 4 servings
> Active time: 30 minutes
> Total time: 1 hour

1½ cups all-purpose flour

½ cup whole wheat flour

1 teaspoon salt

1 teaspoon baking powder

1 teaspoon light or dark brown sugar

2 teaspoons lard or vegetable shortening

¼ cup whole milk or evaporated milk, room temperature

½ cup lukewarm water (or more as needed)

selection of dried chiles, such as guajillo or ancho

1 cup honey

2 quarts peanut oil

1. In a large bowl, combine the flours, salt, baking powder, and brown sugar. Using your fingers, work in the lard or shortening until pea-size lumps form. Add the milk and water and mix with your hands until the dough is sticky and comes together. (Add more water if needed.)

2. On a lightly floured surface, knead the dough for 1 minute; it should be soft and no longer sticky. Let the dough rest, covered with a damp cloth, for at least 15 minutes.

3. Divide the dough into three balls, cover all three with a damp cloth, and let rest for another 15 to 30 minutes.

4. While the dough is resting, make the hot honey. Remove the stems and seeds from the dried chiles, then toast the chiles in a small pan over medium-high heat until fragrant and soft, stirring occasionally. Add the honey to the pan with the softened chiles and cook for at least 10 minutes, then strain the honey with a small strainer into a bowl or jar.

5. On a lightly floured surface, roll out each dough ball into a rectangle approximately ¼ inch thick. Cut the dough using a pizza wheel into 1 to 2-inch wide rectangles. Heat at least 3 inches of peanut oil on medium-high heat in a heavy, high-sided saucepan or skillet to 400°F.

6. Slip 1 or 2 dough pieces into the oil. After sinking briefly, they should begin to balloon and rise to the surface. Once they start floating, carefully spoon oil over them for the few seconds it will take until they have fully puffed. Turn them over and cook until they are just golden, then drain and place on a cooling rack set over a baking sheet. Repeat for the remaining dough.

7. Serve the sopapillas with the hot honey on the side for dipping.

TEQUILA SUNRISE

This three-ingredient cocktail is thought to have been invented by a bartender at the Arizona Biltmore Hotel in the 1930s, but it was in the 1970s that it really took off. Perfect for long gaming nights that are so fun that they turn into game mornings, this colorful cocktail is a great way to greet the dawn with its "sunrise" layers of orange juice, grenadine, and tequila.

Makes: 1 drink
Total time: 5 minutes

1½ ounces (3 tablespoons) blanco tequila

3 ounces (6 tablespoons) freshly squeezed orange juice

½ ounce (1 tablespoon) grenadine or crème de cassis

orange slice, for garnish

maraschino cherry, for garnish

1. Pour the tequila and orange juice directly into a tall glass filled with ice cubes; stir to combine.

2. Tilt the glass and slowly pour in the grenadine down the side of the glass. Allow the grenadine to sink to the bottom for a sunrise effect.

3. Garnish with the orange slice and cherry.

TORTILLA SOUP

Even Tex-Mex doubters can get on board with a good tortilla soup. This broth is a soulful mix of garlic, cumin, chili powder, tomatoes, and masa, made even better by loading it up with black beans and/or chicken. And, of course, no bowl is complete without the namesake tortilla strips tossed on top.

Makes: 4 to 6 servings
Active time: 20 minutes
Total time: 50 minutes

3 tablespoons olive oil, divided

1 onion, diced

2 carrots, peeled and diced

1 jalapeño pepper, diced

2 celery ribs, diced

4 cloves garlic, minced

2 teaspoons ground cumin

2 teaspoons chili powder

1 teaspoon ground oregano

salt and pepper, to taste

1½ pounds boneless, skinless chicken thighs (optional)

1 (14.5-ounce) can diced fire-roasted tomatoes, including juices

1 (15-ounce) can black beans, drained

¼ cup masa harina

4 cups chicken stock

2 cups water

4 corn tortillas

juice of 1 lime

1 avocado, sliced

¼ cup shredded cheddar cheese

¼ cup chopped cilantro

1. Heat 2 tablespoons of olive oil in a large pot over medium-high heat and add the diced onion, carrots, jalapeño, and celery. Cook for 6 to 8 minutes, then add the garlic, cumin, chili powder, oregano, and salt and pepper and cook 30 seconds longer.

2. Next add the chicken thighs (if using), diced tomatoes and juice, black beans, masa harina, chicken stock, and water. Bring to a boil, then reduce heat to medium-low and simmer for 30 minutes.

3. Meanwhile, make the tortilla-strip topping. Heat 1 tablespoon of oil in a large griddle or frying pan over medium-high heat. Cut the tortillas into thin strips and fry in batches until crisp, about 3 to 5 minutes. Remove to a paper-towel-lined plate and sprinkle with salt.

4. Once the soup is done cooking, remove the chicken pieces, if using. Let them cool briefly, then shred the meat and add it back into the soup. Stir in the lime juice, then ladle the soup into bowls and garnish with avocado slices, shredded cheese, the tortilla strips, and cilantro.

Texas-Style Brisket

Texas takes a lot of things seriously, and barbecue is definitely one of them. And brisket? That's pretty much the king of Texas barbecue. But if your train car lacks a smoker, don't worry—this oven version is an almost-as-good substitute that'll still give you that smoky flavor and layer of peppery, sugary "bark."

> Makes: 4 to 6 servings
> Active time: 15 minutes
> Total time: 5 hours 30 minutes

3 to 4 pounds boneless flat-cut beef brisket

2 tablespoons paprika

2 tablespoons light or dark brown sugar

1 tablespoon sea salt

2 teaspoons garlic powder

2 teaspoons onion powder

1 teaspoon black pepper

1 teaspoon cayenne pepper

1 teaspoon ground cumin

½ teaspoon oregano

3 cups water

¼ cup liquid smoke

1. Pat the brisket dry with a paper towel. In a small bowl, whisk together the paprika, brown sugar, salt, garlic powder, onion powder, black pepper, cayenne pepper, cumin, and oregano. Liberally rub the mixture all over the meat. If you have the time and patience, cover and refrigerate the seasoned brisket overnight—but you can also cook it immediately.

2. Preheat the oven to 275°F. Pour the 3 cups of water and the liquid smoke into a large roasting pan. Place the brisket on a wire roasting rack over the water and cover the pan tightly with aluminum foil.

3. Roast for about 1 hour per pound, or until the brisket reaches 180°F. Then turn the oven up to 300°F, remove the foil, and roast until the meat reaches 195°F. Remove from the oven and let rest for at least 30 minutes before serving. Slice against the grain and serve.

CREAMY COLESLAW AND TEXAS TOAST

Texans love their jalapeños and cilantro, so we added them to this for some extra kick! Bring the heat with this must-have barbecue side, perfect for chowing down while your train passes through Texas's beautiful Hill Country. Throw in some thick slabs of Texas toast, and you've got a feast!

Makes: 4 to 6 servings
Active time: 20 minutes
Total time: 2 hours 20 minutes

¾ cup mayonnaise

3 tablespoons apple cider vinegar

1 tablespoon sugar

2 tablespoons fresh lime juice

1 teaspoon kosher salt

¼ teaspoon freshly ground black pepper

2 cups thinly sliced red cabbage

2 cups thinly sliced white cabbage

½ cup shredded carrot

1 jalapeño pepper, finely diced

⅓ cup chopped cilantro

1 loaf thick-cut Texas toast

1. In a large bowl, whisk together the mayonnaise, vinegar, sugar, lime juice, salt, and pepper.

2. Add the cabbages, carrot, and jalapeño and mix well to coat with the dressing. Refrigerate for at least 2 hours.

3. To serve, top the coleslaw with the cilantro. Serve along with the Texas toast.

COWBOY COOKIES

Cowboy cookies are essentially just jazzed-up chocolate chip cookies—and jazzed up they are! The mix of oats, coconut, cinnamon, pecans, and—of course—chocolate chunks is a hearty snack that's perfect for a day spent riding the rails. And since everything is bigger in Texas, feel free to scoop a little more dough than you usually would.

Makes: 24 to 36 cookies
Active time: 15 minutes
Total time: 27 minutes

2 cups flour

1 teaspoon baking soda

1 teaspoon baking powder

½ teaspoon ground cinnamon

1 teaspoon salt

1 cup (2 sticks) unsalted butter, at room temperature

1½ cups packed light brown sugar

½ cup granulated sugar

2 large eggs, at room temperature

1 tablespoon vanilla extract

1¾ cups old-fashioned oats

1 cup sweetened flaked coconut

1 cup halved pecans

1¾ cups (about 8 ounces) semisweet chocolate chunks

1 teaspoon flaky sea salt

1. Preheat the oven to 350°F. In a medium bowl, mix the flour, baking soda, baking powder, cinnamon, and salt.

2. In a large bowl, beat together the butter and sugars with an electric mixer until thoroughly mixed. Add the eggs, one at a time, fully incorporating each one. Mix in the vanilla.

3. Gradually and gently stir in the flour mixture until just combined with a wooden spoon. Then stir in the oats, coconut, pecans, and chocolate.

4. Lightly grease a cookie sheet. Scoop the dough onto the cookie sheet in mounds of 2 to 3 tablespoons and bake for 12 minutes, until just starting to set. While the cookies are still warm, sprinkle the tops with the sea salt, then transfer to a wire rack to cool.

RANCH WATER

Created to beat the scorching Texas heat, Ranch Water is a simple but ultra-refreshing blend of tequila, lime, and sparkling water. That's it. No sugar, just spiked lime water. And if the game with your fellow riders isn't hot enough and you want to raise the heat level, you can add a rim of the spicy Texas favorite, Tajin seasoning!

Makes: 2 drinks
Total time: 5 minutes

Tajin seasoning, for glass rims

4 ounces (½ cup) blanco tequila

2 limes, juiced (for 2 tablespoons), plus wedges for garnish

8 ounces (1 cup) sparkling water, such as Topo Chico

1. Rim two glasses with the Tajin seasoning, then fill each of them with ice.

2. Pour in half the tequila, lime juice, and sparkling water into each glass.

3. Stir and then garnish with the lime wedges.

Did You Know?
Ticket to Ride is fun for the whole family but recommended for ages 8 and up. If you have little ones who love trains, check out Ticket to Ride: First Journey.

COAST TO COAST

VANCOUVER ◆ MONTREAL

BEAVER TAILS WITH REAL MAPLE SYRUP

Beaver tails are a popular Canadian treat made of deep-fried, sweetened dough dusted with spiced sugar. They get their name because of the way the dough looks when stretched and fried, resembling a beaver's flat, broad tail. These beloved treats are best enjoyed at festivals, fairs, and while blocking your fellow passengers' train routes.

Makes: 6 servings
Active time: 20 minutes
Total time: 1 hour 20 minutes

½ cup warm water

5 teaspoons active dry yeast

⅓ cup plus ¼ teaspoon sugar, divided

1 cup whole milk

1 teaspoon salt

1 teaspoon vanilla extract

2 eggs

⅓ cup vegetable oil

5 cups flour

2 quarts neutral oil for frying, such as peanut

FOR DUSTING

½ cup sugar

1 teaspoon ground cinnamon

¼ teaspoon freshly ground nutmeg

¼ teaspoon ground cloves

⅛ teaspoon ground chipotle chili powder

SPECIAL EQUIPMENT

stand mixer with a dough hook

deep fryer

1. Make the dusting sugar by mixing ½ cup sugar with the cinnamon, nutmeg, cloves, and ground chipotle in a small bowl; set aside.

2. In a large bowl, mix the warm water, yeast, and ¼ teaspoon sugar. Let stand a couple of minutes to let the yeast swell and dissolve.

3. Add the ⅓ cup sugar, milk, salt, vanilla, eggs, vegetable oil, and most of the flour to the yeast mixture. Knead for 5 to 8 minutes using the dough hook attachment of an electric mixer, adding more flour as needed to form a firm, smooth, elastic dough. Place the dough in a lightly greased bowl, cover, and set in a warm spot to rise for 1 hour.

4. Pinch off a piece of dough the size of a golf ball. On a floured surface, roll it into a ¼-inch oval and let it rest, covered with a tea towel, while you prepare the remaining dough the same way.

5. In a deep fryer or medium pot, heat the oil to 375°F. Add the dough pieces to the hot oil one at a time, using tongs to turn each beaver tail once and frying until both sides are deep brown, about 1 to 2 minutes per side.

6. Lift out with the tongs and drain on paper towels. While warm, toss the beaver tails in the sugar mixture, coating both sides and shaking off the excess.

POUTINE

When you top crispy french fries with cheese curds and gravy, you're going to win some fans. And while poutine is Canada's national dish—and probably the best known—this messy, meaty, cheesy pile of goodness can be found in cities all across the map.

Makes: 4 to 6 servings
Active time: 1 hour
Total time: 1 hour 30 minutres

FRIES
4 large russet potatoes

2 quarts peanut oil

1 tablespoon sea salt

1 teaspoon freshly cracked pepper

1 teaspoon dried thyme

GRAVY
4 tablespoons (½ stick) unsalted butter

¼ cup flour

¾ teaspoon garlic powder

½ teaspoon onion powder

1 teaspoon smoked paprika

1 teaspoon herbs de Provence or dried thyme

1 teaspoon salt

1 teaspoon pepper

1 cup chicken broth

1 cup beef broth

1½ teaspoons Worcestershire sauce

1 beef bouillon cube

1 teaspoon unfiltered apple cider vinegar

1. To prepare the fries, peel and cut the potatoes into ⅓-inch-wide strips, the length of the potato. Place in a large bowl and rinse with cold water until the water runs clear. Soak for at least 30 minutes, or up to 24 hours for crispier fries.

2. While the potatoes soak, make the gravy. In a large saucepan set over medium heat, cook the butter and flour together, stirring constantly with a wooden spoon until golden brown, about 2 minutes. Then stir in the garlic powder, onion powder, paprika, herbs de Provence or thyme, salt, and pepper. Drizzle in the chicken and beef broths, being careful to work slowly to keep lumps from forming.

3. Increase the heat to medium-high and bring the mixture to a boil, stirring often. Then reduce the heat to low and simmer until thickened, about 10 to 15 minutes, stirring occasionally. Stir in the Worcestershire sauce, beef bouillon, and vinegar. Season with salt and pepper.

4. For the fries, remove the potato strips from the water and thoroughly dry them with paper towels. Pour the peanut oil into a large, heavy-bottomed pot and heat over medium-high heat until the oil reaches 300°F.

5. Working in batches, fry the potato slices for 5 to 6 minutes. Remove from the oil with a spider strainer and increase the heat until the oil reaches 400°F. Fry the potatoes a second time in batches until golden brown, about 5 minutes. Remove and place on a baking sheet lined with paper towels. Immediately sprinkle with salt, pepper, and thyme.

FOR SERVING

10 ounces white cheddar cheese curds, at room temperature

6 strips thick-cut bacon, cooked and crumbled

¼ cup caramelized onions (see note)

minced fresh parsley, for garnish

6. To assemble the poutine, transfer fries to a serving dish. Start with a base of fries. Sprinkle with the cheese curds, drizzle on the gravy, and top with the bacon crumbles and caramelized onions. Garnish with minced parsley and serve hot.

Note
See step 1 of the Cheese Crisps recipe on page 127.

Split Pea Soup

A hearty soup is perfect for Canada's cold weather, and this spin on traditional split pea soup will get your game night on track. Crispy speck or bacon chips and a drizzle of mint oil take the bowls to the next level, adding some zip and bite to this comforting soup.

Makes: 6 servings
Active time: 25 minutes
Total time: 1 hour 30 minutes

6 ounces speck (cured, smoked ham) or bacon

2 celery ribs, finely diced

1 yellow onion, finely diced

2 carrots, peeled and finely diced

3 cloves garlic, minced

1 teaspoon ground cumin

1 teaspoon smoked paprika

½ teaspoon mustard powder

1 tablespoon salt

1 tablespoon freshly cracked black pepper

1½ teaspoons Worcestershire sauce

1 tablespoon soy sauce

4 cups chicken stock

4 cups water

1-pound bag split peas

mint leaves (about 20)

⅓ cup neutral oil, such as canola or avocado

1. In a large, heavy-bottomed pot over medium-high heat, cook your speck or bacon pieces until crispy. Remove and set aside on paper towels.

2. Add the celery, onion, and carrots to the pot with the meat, sautéing until beginning to brown, about 6 to 8 minutes, stirring occasionally. Add the garlic, cumin, paprika, mustard powder, and salt and pepper and cook for 1 minute, until fragrant. Add the Worcestershire sauce, soy sauce, chicken stock, and water, scraping up any brown bits from the bottom of the pan.

3. Add the split peas and bring to a boil. Then reduce the heat to low and simmer for an hour, until the peas are tender.

4. While the soup is cooking, add the mint leaves to a blender with the oil. Blend on high until fully incorporated, about 30 seconds. Strain the mint oil through a fine mesh strainer and set aside.

5. When the soup is done cooking, remove it from the heat and use a potato masher to break up some of the peas for a more velvety texture. Ladle into bowls and top each serving with speck or bacon crumbles and a drizzle of mint oil.

Maple-Glazed Smoked Salmon

As in the Pacific Northwest region of the US, Canadians smoke salmon to preserve the fish over the long, rough winters. Combining the rich, smoky flavor of the salmon with the sweet, earthy taste of maple syrup, this recipe is a distractingly delicious entrée that might give you an advantage over other players sidetracked by this show stopper.

Makes: 6 servings
Active time: 30 minutes
Total time: 4 hours 30 minutes

½ cup kosher salt

1 cup dark brown sugar

⅔ cup quality maple syrup, divided

¼ cup soy sauce

2 tablespoons Worcestershire sauce

3 cloves garlic

1 tablespoon grated fresh ginger

½ cup water

6 (6-ounce) salmon fillets

3 green onions, chopped

2 tablespoons sesame seeds

SPECIAL EQUIPMENT
hot smoker

1. In a small saucepan, stir together the salt, sugar, ⅓ cup maple syrup, soy sauce, Worcestershire sauce, whole garlic cloves, ginger, and water. Cook over low heat until the sugar and salt are dissolved, then remove from the stovetop and let cool.

2. Fill a large ziplock bag with the cooled marinade. Submerge the salmon fillets in the marinade, seal, and refrigerate for at least 2 hours.

3. Preheat your hot smoker to 200°F and line a tray with parchment paper. Remove the fish from the marinade, pat dry with paper towels, and place skin side down on the tray.

4. Place the fish in the smoker. Baste with the remaining ⅓ cup maple syrup every 30 minutes for 2 hours, until the fish reaches an internal temperature of 140°F.

5. Slice the salmon and garnish with chopped green onions and sesame seeds to serve.

BANNOCK

This tender, mildly sweet bread blends the cuisines of Canada's First Nations people and Scottish settlers. The dough comes together easily and puffs up with a quick fry, making for a versatile snack to fuel your adventures across the continent.

Makes: 6 servings
Active time: 30 minutes
Total time: 40 minutes

1¾ cups all-purpose flour

¼ cup whole wheat flour

1 teaspoon kosher salt

1 tablespoon dark brown sugar

2 teaspoons baking powder

2 tablespoons plus 2 quarts vegetable oil, divided

¾ cup water

1. In a large bowl, whisk together the flours, salt, brown sugar, and baking powder.

2. Add the 2 tablespoons oil and mix in with your hands until evenly distributed. Drizzle in the water as needed until the dough begins to come together. Move to a lightly floured flat surface and knead 12 times; the dough will be sticky, but do not overmix. Let rest for 5 to 10 minutes.

3. Add enough vegetable oil to a large cast-iron skillet to shallowly cover the bottom, about 1 inch. Set over medium heat to let the oil reach 350°F.

4. Divide the dough into six equal balls and flatten each with the palm of your hand. Gently place in the oil and fry in batches until golden brown on both sides, 1 to 2 minutes per side. Drain on a baking sheet lined with paper towels.

Nanaimo Bar

Named for British Columbia's city of Nanaimo, this no-bake dessert consists of three layers: a nutty crumb base, a creamy custard middle, and a smooth chocolate top. The first known recipe for Nanaimo bars was published in a local cookbook in the 1950s, and since then their popularity has been full steam ahead. This recipe enhances the classic with the added richness of maple syrup, brown butter, and espresso.

Makes: 8 servings
Active time: 30 minutes
Total time: 1 hour

DESSERT BASE

½ cup (1 stick) unsalted butter

¼ cup dark brown sugar

5 tablespoons unsweetened cocoa powder

½ teaspoon salt

1 large egg, lightly beaten

1¾ cups graham cracker crumbs

½ cup finely chopped pecans

1 cup unsweetened, finely shredded coconut

FILLING

½ cup (1 stick) unsalted butter

3 tablespoons custard powder

2 teaspoons vanilla extract

1 tablespoon maple syrup

2 cups powdered sugar

4 tablespoons (¼ cup) heavy cream, plus 1 to 2 more teaspoons, if needed

1. To make brown butter for the filling, add ½ cup butter to a small saucepan and cook slowly over medium-low heat until foamy, golden brown, and smelling like toasted nuts, about 5 to 10 minutes. Remove from the heat to let cool completely and solidify.

2. Grease a 9-inch square pan and line with a parchment paper sling, leaving an overhang on opposite sides for easy removal of the bars.

3. To make the base, heat a medium saucepan of water to a gentle simmer over medium-low heat, then melt another ½ cup butter in a large heatproof bowl set over the saucepan. Whisk in the brown sugar, cocoa powder, and salt. Remove from the heat and slowly add in the egg, whisking vigorously. Return to the heat over the saucepan and cook for 1 to 2 more minutes, until the mixture is smooth and resembles hot fudge.

4. Add the graham cracker crumbs, pecans, and shredded coconut. Stir until the mixture is well combined and holds its shape if pressed. Transfer the graham cracker mixture to the prepared pan. Press it firmly and evenly into the bottom of the pan and place in the refrigerator to chill while you prepare the next layer.

5. In a large mixing bowl, beat together the cooled brown butter, custard powder, vanilla, and maple syrup for the filling until well combined. Mix in the powdered sugar and add the ¼ cup cream, 1 tablespoon at a time, until you achieve a thick but spreadable consistency.

6. Spread the filling evenly over the base layer (an offset spatula works well for this). Place in the freezer for 10 to 15 minutes to firm while you prepare the next layer.

GANACHE

8 ounces dark chocolate, chopped

3 tablespoons heavy cream, or 4 tablespoons if using espresso powder

1 shot espresso or 1 tablespoon espresso powder

2 teaspoons flaky sea salt

7. For the ganache, combine the chocolate, 3 tablespoons cream, and espresso in a medium heatproof bowl over the saucepan of simmering water, stirring frequently, until the chocolate is completely melted and the mixture is smooth.

8. Pour the chocolate mixture over the chilled buttercream and quickly spread, using an offset spatula. Sprinkle with flaky sea salt and place back in the fridge for at least 15 minutes. Remove from the pan and cut into 8 pieces to serve.

CAESAR COCKTAIL

Canada's version of a Bloody Mary swaps clamato for tomato juice, making for a saltier sip. And just as in the US, garnishes are loved. Canada gussies up the drink with everything from bacon strips to celery ribs. If you're holding a few locomotive cards, get wild with the accoutrements and see why this is Canada's national cocktail.

Makes: 2 drinks
Total time: 5 minutes

celery salt, to rim the glasses
pepper, to rim the glasses
3 ounces (6 tablespoons) vodka
8 ounces (1 cup) clamato juice
5 dashes hot sauce
5 dashes Worcestershire sauce
lime wedges, celery ribs, and
stuffed green olives, for garnish

1. Rim two tall glasses with celery salt and pepper, then fill with ice.

2. Fill a separate mixing glass with ice, then add the vodka, clamato juice, hot sauce, and Worcestershire. Pour back and forth into another glass to gently mix.

3. Strain the drink into the rimmed glasses and garnish with lime wedges, celery, green olives (on toothpicks or cocktail picks)—and whatever else your heart desires.

COAST TO COAST

Tater Tot Hotdish

Tater tots were dreamed up in the 1950s at an Oregon potato plant as a way to use up rogue potato shavings left over after making french fries. Soon these squat little fry byproducts became a craving all on their own—and this breakfast version of the classic Midwest casserole with eggs, ham, and cheese (or breakfast for dinner, if you've got an evening game going) ups the comfort factor even more.

Makes: 8 servings
Active time: 10 minutes
Total time: 1 hour

1 tablespoon olive oil

1 red bell pepper, diced

1 onion, diced

1 (32-ounce) bag frozen tater tots

8 ounces diced cooked ham

1 cup shredded cheddar cheese, divided

1⅓ cups shredded gruyère and swiss cheese mixture

8 large eggs

½ cup whole milk

½ cup sour cream

½ teaspoon each salt and pepper

½ teaspoon garlic powder

3 green onions, sliced

1. Preheat the oven to 375°F. Grease a 9 x13-inch baking dish with butter or cooking spray. In a medium skillet over medium-high heat, combine the olive oil, bell pepper, and onion and cook for 5 minutes, or until just tender.

2. Place the diced pepper and onions in the baking dish with the tater tots, ham, ½ cup cheddar, and all the gruyère and swiss cheese; stir to combine.

3. In a large bowl, whisk together the eggs, milk, sour cream, salt, pepper, and garlic powder. Pour the mixture over the tater tots.

4. Bake for 45 minutes, until the eggs are set and the tots are golden brown. Then top with the remaining ½ cup of cheddar and bake for 5 more minutes. Top with the green onions and serve.

VEGGIE BURGER

This burger might be a little more work than its meat counterpart, but the result is well worth the effort. You get layers of flavor from the roasted veggies, a hit of umami from the mushrooms, and satisfying heartiness from the brown rice. Top it all off with sauce inspired by a certain West Coast burger chain and you've got an incredible-tasting American icon that will satisfy vegetarian and carnivorous riders alike.

Makes: 6 burgers
Active time: 1 hour
Total time: 1 hour 25 minutes

8 ounces mushrooms, roughly chopped

1 carrot, roughly chopped

½ yellow onion, roughly chopped

3 cloves garlic

2 tablespoons olive oil

1 teaspoon chili powder

1 teaspoon paprika

½ teaspoon ground cumin

½ teaspoon salt

pepper, to taste

1 (15-ounce) can black beans, drained

1 cup raw spinach

¼ cup chopped chives

⅔ cup panko breadcrumbs

2 eggs

1 tablespoon tomato paste

2 tablespoons vegan Worcestershire sauce

⅔ cup cooked brown rice

½ cup mayonnaise

3 tablespoons ketchup

2 tablespoons sweet pickle relish

6 burger buns

1. Preheat the oven to 375°F. Place the mushrooms, carrot, and onion in a food processor with the garlic, olive oil, chili powder, paprika, cumin, salt, and pepper. Pulse until the mixture has a paste-like texture.

2. Line a baking sheet with foil and spread the veggie mixture over half the surface. Roast in the oven for about 15 minutes.

3. Add the drained black beans to the other half of the baking sheet, then place the pan back in the oven for another 10 minutes, until the beans begin to crack.

4. Place the spinach, chives, and roasted black beans in the food processor. Pulse a few times, then add the roasted vegetable mixture, panko crumbs, eggs, tomato paste, and Worcestershire sauce. Pulse until just combined.

5. Place the mixture in a large bowl and stir in your cooked brown rice. When you're ready to cook the burgers, form the mixture into patties and cook in a large frying pan over medium-high heat, 4 to 6 minutes per side.

6. To make the sauce, mix the mayonnaise, ketchup, and pickle relish in a small bowl. Assemble your burgers with sauce and any favorite toppings.

BUFFALO CHICKEN DIP

For those hotshots out there, this dip is the perfect game-day accompaniment. Serve it as an early-afternoon appetizer, a late-night snack, or even a well-balanced meal (if using carrots and celery sticks to scoop up every last drop of spicy, creamy goodness is considered well balanced). Inspired by the iconic wings from Anchor Bar in Buffalo, New York, this is the dip for those who like to feel the heat!

Makes: 6 servings
Active time: 10 minutes
Total time: 25 minutes

2 cups shredded cooked chicken

½ cup hot sauce

8 ounces cream cheese, softened

½ cup ranch dressing

½ cup shredded cheddar cheese

¼ cup crumbled blue cheese

¼ cup chopped green onions, green and white parts

carrot and celery sticks, for dipping

1. Preheat the oven to 350°F. In a large bowl, mix together the chicken, hot sauce, cream cheese, and ranch dressing.

2. Pour the mixture into an 8-inch cast-iron skillet or ovenproof dish. Sprinkle the cheddar cheese on top. Bake for 15 minutes, or until the mixture is heated through and the cheese is bubbling.

3. Remove from the oven, top with the blue cheese crumbles and green onions, and serve with carrot and celery sticks for dipping.

TURKEY BLUE PLATE SPECIAL

All aboard the gravy train! Served in diners across North America since the 1800s, blue plate specials fill you up without breaking the bank. A turkey blue plate special is one of the most iconic, and one of the most satisfying. This one tops sous-vide-cooked turkey with creamy mashed potatoes and a hearty gravy.

Makes: 8 servings
Active time: 1 hour
Total time: 4 hours

TURKEY AND GRAVY

1 bone-in turkey breast, defrosted if frozen

3 cups chicken broth

1 tablespoon garlic powder

3 tablespoons plus 2 teaspoons kosher salt, divided

1 teaspoon freshly cracked pepper

2 tablespoons plus 1 teaspoon herbs de Provence, divided

1 teaspoon dark brown sugar

4 tablespoons (½ stick) unsalted butter

3 tablespoons flour

2 cloves garlic, minced

2 teaspoons smoked paprika

POTATOES

6 large russet potatoes

2 tablespoons kosher salt, or as needed

1 cup (2 sticks) unsalted butter

1 cup half-and-half

½ teaspoon freshly ground nutmeg

1. To prepare the turkey breast, begin by removing the bones with a boning knife, cutting around the bottom bone in long, slow slices to release the breast. Add the bones to a large pot with the 3 cups chicken broth. Bring to a boil over medium-high heat, then reduce to a low simmer and cook for at least 30 minutes. This is the stock for your gravy.

2. Make a spice rub for the turkey by combining the garlic powder, 3 tablespoons salt, 1 tablespoon pepper, 2 tablespoons herbs de Provence, and brown sugar. Roll the deboned turkey breast into a log, making it as uniform in thickness as possible. Generously pat on the spice mix and then place the turkey in a 2-gallon freezer bag.

3. Using an immersion circulator (sous vide machine) set to 145°F, place the bag in the water bath to cook the breast for 2½ hours. The turkey will be tender and moist; this is the best way to cook the lean meat. (If you do not have an immersion circulator, place the breast on a baking pan and roast in the oven at 375°F until the internal temperature reaches 145°F, about 30 to 40 minutes. Since you will be roasting the turkey, there is no need for Step 6, browning it in a pan.)

4. While the turkey is cooking, prepare the mashed potatoes. Peel and cut the potatoes into 1-inch squares. Add to a large pot of boiling water and cook for 10 to 12 minutes, until tender. Use a colander to drain the potatoes and then return them to the dry pan.

SPECIAL EQUIPMENT
sous vide immersion circulator
(optional)
ricer or food mill

5. In a separate medium saucepan, combine the 2 tablespoons salt, 2 sticks butter, half-and-half, and nutmeg over medium heat, stirring occasionally until the mixture begins to simmer. Remove from the heat. Push the cooked potatoes through a ricer or food mill into a large bowl and then fold in the dairy mixture. If needed, season with extra salt.

6. Once the turkey is cooked, remove it from the plastic bag and pat dry with paper towels. In a large sauté pan, melt 4 tablespoons butter over medium-high heat. Add the turkey breast and cook for 2 to 3 minutes on each side, until golden brown. Remove from the pan and let rest on a cutting board.

7. To make the gravy, combine the 3 tablespoons flour with the butter already in the sauté pan and cook for 4 minutes, stirring occasionally. Stir in the minced garlic, 2 teaspoons salt, 1 teaspoon pepper, 1 teaspoon herbs de Provence, and paprika, then cook for an additional minute. Remove the bones from the stock, then slowly incorporate the stock into the butter-flour mixture, stirring continuously to avoid lumps.

8. Slice the turkey breast and serve on a platter over a bed of mashed potatoes drizzled with gravy.

> ### Did You Know?
> Ticket to Ride is not the only hit game from creator Alan R. Moon. His 1998 game Elfenland also won the prestigious Spiel des Jahres award.

Cornbread, Sausage, and Sage Stuffing

Synonymous with Thanksgiving, stuffing—or dressing, as it's often called in the South—is an American comfort food staple. This savory hodgepodge of bread, meat, vegetables, and spices is so distractingly good that you just might be able to block your fellow passengers' routes between bites. The Cornbread, Sausage, and Sage Stuffing presented here is made even better when topped with Turkey Blue Plate Special gravy (page 171).

Makes: 8 servings
Active time: 35 minutes
Total time: 1 hour 35 minutes

1 pound ground Italian sausage or links, casings removed

½ cup (1 stick) unsalted butter, divided

2 leeks, chopped in ¼-inch pieces

2 onions, chopped in ¼-inch pieces

2 carrots, chopped in ¼-inch pieces

3 celery ribs, chopped in ¼-inch pieces

2 red peppers, chopped in ¼-inch pieces

8 cloves garlic, minced

store-bought cornbread (or you can make your own)

2 cups chicken stock

2 eggs

2 tablespoons salt

1 tablespoon pepper

1 tablespoon herbs de Provence

1. In a large pan over medium-high heat, brown the sausage and then remove it from the pan, leaving the fat from the sausage in the pan. Add ¼ cup butter (half a stick) and the chopped leeks, onions, carrots, celery, and red peppers, stirring occasionally. Cook until slightly brown, about 8 to 10 minutes. Stir in the garlic and cook until fragrant, about 1 minute. Remove from the heat to cool.

2. While the veggies are cooking, preheat the oven to 400°F. Cube the cornbread in 1-inch pieces and place in a bowl. Melt the remaining ¼ cup butter in a small pan over medium-high heat and then drizzle it over the cornbread. Spread evenly onto a rimmed baking sheet and bake for 15 to 20 minutes, until the bread is brown and crisp. Remove and let cool.

3. In a separate large bowl, whisk together the chicken stock, eggs, salt, pepper, herbs de Provence, nutmeg, and chipotle powder or paprika. Add the cooled cornbread, sausage, and sautéed vegetables and fold together, being careful not to break up the cornbread too much.

4. Pour the stuffing into a greased baking dish and top with the toasted pecans. Bake uncovered for 30 to 45 minutes, until the top is golden and the stuffing is cooked through and a digital thermometer reads 165°F. Remove from the oven and let sit for at least 10 minutes before serving.

1 teaspoon freshly ground nutmeg

1 tablespoon chipotle powder or smoked paprika

½ cup pecans, toasted

¼ cup canola oil

10 sage leaves

5. While the stuffing is resting, add the canola oil to a small sauté pan over medium-high heat. Heat until shimmering, about 3 minutes, then add the fresh sage leaves and fry for about 20 seconds. (Be careful—they will splatter.) Transfer to a paper-towel-lined plate to drain, then arrange the sage leaves on top of your stuffing as a garnish.

APPLE PIE

"As American as apple pie" is a well-used colloquialism—and really, what nation wouldn't want to be associated with buttery pie crust and slow-cooked apples flavored with cinnamon and sugar? This classic recipe ups the salt a bit—in the filling and via a generous sprinkling on top of the domed crust—for a salty-sweet flavor combo that's as American as you know what.

Makes: 1 (9-inch) pie
Active time: 40 minutes
Total time: 2 hours 55 minutes

CRUST

2½ cups unbleached flour, chilled

1 tablespoon sugar

1 teaspoon salt

1 cup (2 sticks) unsalted butter, cubed and cold

1 large egg, lightly beaten

cold water, as needed

FILLING

4 large apples (about 5 cups, peled and thinly sliced)— Jonathan, Fuji, Cortland, or Golden Delicious

1 to 2 tablespoons lemon juice

⅔ cup sugar

1 teaspoon salt

¼ cup flour

¼ teaspoon ground cinnamon

1 tablespoon unsalted butter, cut into small pieces

1 beaten egg, for brushing on crust

sugar (granulated or turbinado), for sprinkling

sea salt, for sprinkling

1. To make the crust, in a medium bowl whisk together the flour, sugar, and salt. Using a bench scraper, large metal spoons, or a food processor with metal blades, cut the cubed butter into the mixture until it is in small, pea-sized chunks.

2. Stir in the egg with a fork, or mix with a food processor. If the dough is too dry, add cold water a tablespoon at a time. You want the dough to be moist enough to just hold together when pinched.

3. Cut the dough in half and form into 2 disks. Cover each disk tightly with plastic wrap and refrigerate for at least 1 hour.

4. Preheat the oven to 375°F. Dust a clean work surface with flour and roll each dough disk into a 12-inch circle about ⅛ inch thick. Butter a 9-inch pie pan and line it with one of the dough disks; trim the overhang to about 1 inch. Line the crust with parchment paper topped with pie weights and bake for 10 minutes.

5. Meanwhile, make the filling. Place the apples in a medium bowl. Toss with enough lemon juice to lightly coat the slices. Pour in the sugar, salt, flour, and cinnamon and gently toss.

6. Pour the apple filling into the pie shell, making a small mound in the center. Top with the butter pieces. Brush the egg onto the crust edges, then place the second dough disk on top. Roll the top and bottom dough edges together to seal, then crimp to your liking. Use a knife to make 4 to 6 slashes in the center for venting, brush the top with the beaten egg, and sprinkle with sugar and salt.

7. Bake for 50 minutes, until the crust is golden. Remove to a cooling rack for 15 to 30 minutes. Serve warm.

Gold Rush Sour

The Gold Rush Sour gives all the warmth of a hot toddy without the, well, warmth. While you will need some heat to make the honey syrup, this is a drink served chilled. You'll be sipping this classic combo of whiskey, lemon, and honey until last call in the bar car.

> Make 2 drinks
> Active time: 5 minutes
> Total time: 25 minutes

½ cup honey

½ cup water

4 ounces (½ cup) bourbon whiskey

2 ounces (¼ cup) fresh lemon juice

lemon slices, for garnish

1. In a small saucepan over high heat, bring the honey and water to a light boil. Whisk together and remove the honey syrup from the heat to cool.

2. In a cocktail shaker filled with ice, pour 2 ounces (¼ cup) honey syrup, the bourbon, and the lemon juice. Shake until frothy and well chilled, about 30 seconds.

3. Strain into rocks glasses filled with ice, and garnish with lemon slices.

CONVERSIONS

VOLUME

US	US EQUIVALENT	METRIC
1 tablespoon (3 teaspoons)	½ fluid ounce	15 milliliters
¼ cup	2 fluid ounces	60 milliliters
⅓ cup	3 fluid ounces	90 milliliters
½ cup	4 fluid ounces	120 milliliters
⅔ cup	5 fluid ounces	150 milliliters
¾ cup	6 fluid ounces	180 milliliters
1 cup	8 fluid ounces	240 milliliters
2 cups	16 fluid ounces	480 milliliters

WEIGHT

US	METRIC
½ ounce	15 grams
1 ounce	30 grams
2 ounces	60 grams
¼ pound	115 grams
⅓ pound	150 grams
½ pound	225 grams
¾ pound	350 grams
1 pound	450 grams

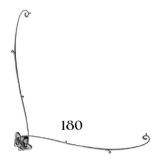

TEMPERATURE

FAHRENHEIT (°F)	CELSIUS (°C)
70°F	20°C
100°F	40°C
120°F	50°C
130°F	55°C
140°F	60°C
150°F	65°C
160°F	70°C
170°F	75°C
180°F	80°C
190°F	90°C
200°F	95°C
220°F	105°C
240°F	115°C
260°F	125°C
280°F	140°C
300°F	150°C
325°F	165°C
350°F	175°C
375°F	190°C
400°F	200°C
425°F	220°C
450°F	230°C

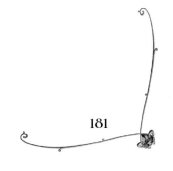

Recipe Index

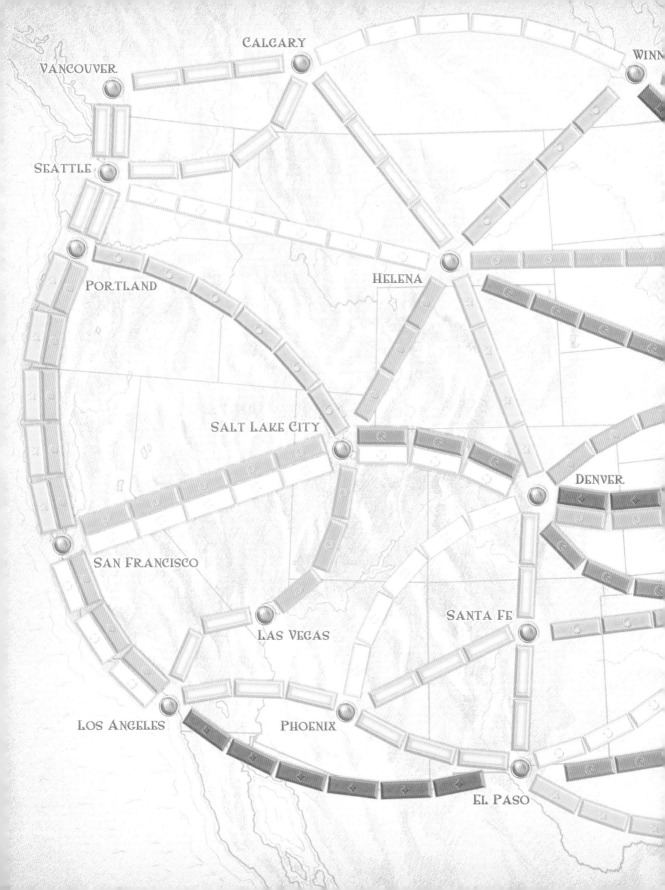

TICKET TO RIDE®

 Scan the code to get the game!

 Marmalade GAME STUDIO